Ancient Egyptian Medicine

C. Savona-Ventura

2017

© Charles Savona-Ventura
Malta, 2017

All rights reserved
[originally published as a series of articles in *Synapse, Hera, Treasures of Malta and Malta Medical Journal*]

Published by Lulu.com

ISBN: 978-0-244-33501-4

Contents

Fertility and Childbirth 5

Surgery 15

Microscopy in the Pharaonic Period 23

Medicine and therapeutics 27

Medical papyri 31

Reproductive issues in the Torah 41

Punic & Egyptian Remains from Malta 61

Classical sources on Mummification 97

Fertility and Childbirth

The Ancient Egyptians with their belief in the afterlife left detailed representations of their way of life in the various contemporary inscriptions and pictograms left in their tombs and temples. A tour of the various sites in Egypt will allow for a visual resume of various aspects of life in Ancient Egypt ranging from daily activities to leisure. There are in addition several aspects related to health and medicine.

Bearing children is an essential *sine qua non* for the continuation of the community. This important requisite resulted in the development of protective deities such as Bes and Thouris. There was also an attempt to understand and manage the reproductive process.

An intriguing relief in the Barque Chamber at Luxor Temple dedicated to the Theban Triad of Amon, Mut, and Chons shows the pharaoh collecting the "essence of life" from the ithy-phallic deity fertility deity Amon-Ra, creator of the universe. The subsequent relief in the series shows the pharaoh presenting his offering to the diety. This latter relief depicts the deity with an erect phallus exuding sperm. A close-up view of this relief identifies a spermatozoon-like structure in relation to the semen flow. The availability of magnification to the Egyptians is not surprising in the light of the discovery of a number of lenses dated to the 3rd century BC. One such crystal lens, discovered in Karanis, Egypt between 1924 and 1929, is kept in the Cairo Egyptian Museum. The fine grinding of rock crystal to produce lenses in Egypt however dates significantly earlier to the IV Dynasty (3rd millennium BC) as evidenced by the numerous number ground rock-crystal eyes found in statutes dated to that period. These include the inlaid eyes found in the Nofret statute from Maydun and the seated scribe statute from Saqqara both in the Cairo Museum. These ground rock-crystal lenses have a convex surface and a flat base, except for a central concavity in the region of the pupil. These lenses confirm that the Egyptians had the necessary technology to manufacture optic-based instruments, including a high resolution magnifying glass suitable for studying microscopic structures.

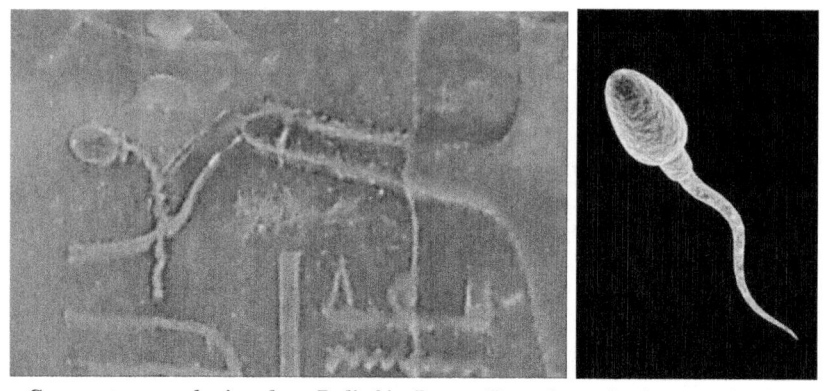

Spermatozoon depicted on Relief in Luxor Temple and microscopic view

Detailed information relating to gynaecological problems and their management in Ancient Egypt is documented in the Kahun Gynaecological Papyrus [for transcribed text see *http://www.reshafim.org.il/ad/egypt/timelines/topics/kahunpapyrus.htm*]. The

Kahun Papyrus, housed in the University College London, is dated to this period by a note on the recto which states the date as being the 29th year of the reign of Amenenhat III (c. 1825 B.C.E.).

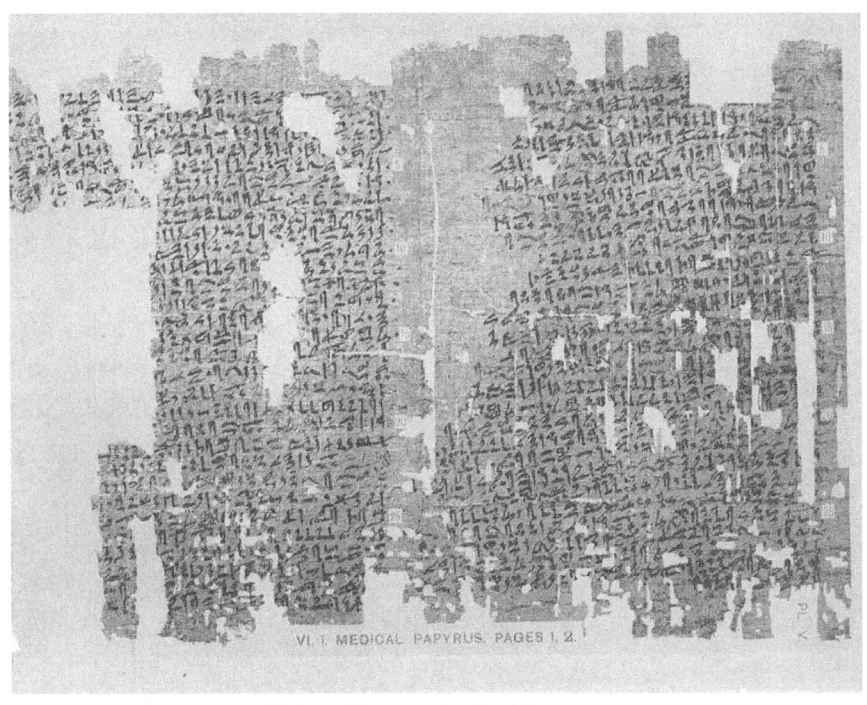

Kahun Gynaecological Papyrus

According to the Kahun Papyrus, fertility in the female was tested by placing an onion bulb in the vagina overnight and identifying the odour in the patient's nose the next day [*para.28*]. Contraception was achieved by using crocodile dung, 45ml of honey, and sour milk [*para. 21-23*]. The Ebers Papyrus gives different contraceptive remedies: "*To cause a woman to stop being pregnant,* be it one, two or three years: *part of acacia, colocynth, dates, finely ground in a hin of honey, fibers are moistened therewith, introduced into her vagina*". To assist pregnancy: *after ceases the return .... pound, grind fine, [strain] in cloth on gruel auyt, pour mehuyu .... Incense, fresh fat, dates, sweet beer, put inside a rack (of wood) in the flame; thou shalt fumigate .... as a sweetener of the mouth* [*Kahun papyrus, para.20*].

Diagnosis of pregnancy was made on the ability of pregnant urine to germinate cereals: *Means for knowing if a woman will give birth or will not give birth: (Put) some barley and some wheat (into two bags of cloth) which the woman will moisten with her urine every day, equally barley and grain in the two bags. If both the barley and the wheat sprout she will give birth. If (only) the barley germinates it will be a boy, if it is the wheat which alone germinates it will be a girl. If neither germinates she will not give birth* [*Berlin papyrus 3.038*].

Abortions were carried out by the introduction of warm oil and fat in the vagina. The Ebers papyrus mentions two remedies which "*cause all to come out which is in the stomach of a woman*", possibly referring to inducing a miscarriage. Delivery was performed in the squatting position as depicted in the frieze in the Sobek temple at Kom Ombo. Assistance was furnished by midwives, two of whom are known by name – Shiphrah and Puah [*Exodus: 1:15-16*]. Difficult labours were aided by burning resin, or massaging the abdomen by saffron powder and beer. Obstructed labour gave rise to serious complications including the development of vesico-vaginal fistulae [*Kahun papyrus, para.35*]. The mummy of Queen Henhenit dated to 2050 BC was found to have such a fistula which was most likely caused by obstructed labour causing also her death. The prognostic signs of survival of the newborn were detailed by the Ebers Papyrus: *Another way of knowing about a child the day he is born: If he says ny, this means he will live. If he says mhj, this means his death. Another way of knowing: When one hears his voice groan, this means his death. If he turns his face downwards, this too means death* [*para. 839-839*].

The goddess Ritho giving birth to the god Ra assisted by midwives

Assisted birth using birthing stool assisted by attendants

Birth Relief at Sobek Temple

Birth on haunches using birthing bricks

Birthing brick

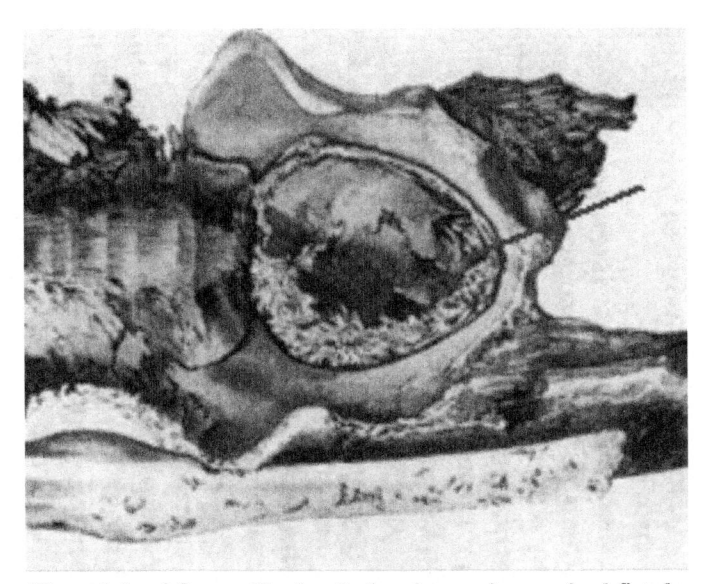

The pelvis of Queen Henhenit showing vesico-vaginal fistula.

Mammisi or birth houses were annexed to temples, but these served to request divine help by pregnant women rather than being a birthing place. Deity protectors of the parturient woman were Taweret and Bes. Taweret was depicted with the head of a hippopotamus, the legs and arms of a lion, the tail of a crocodile, human breasts, and a swollen belly. She was often depicted holding the Sa amulet symbolizing protection. Bes was depicted as a dwarf with ugly features. The appearance was meant to frighten off any spirits that might be harmful to the child.

Bes edifgy   *Taweret edifgy*   *Isis breastfeeding Horus*

Mothers were encouraged to breastfeed their infants for three years *"Nothing is more lawful than one's mother milk"*. The mother deity Isis was repeatedly depicted breastfeeding her son Horus. Infants were generally breastfed for three years, and the Ebers Papyrus describes the use of milk stimulants: *"To bring forth the milk of a nurse who feeds sbj: who must feed a child: Spine of Nile-perch, fried in oil/fat, her spine is anointed therewith"*. When breastfeeding failed resort was made to cow's milk. The breastfeeding mother had further recourse to the deity Taweret.

There can be no doubt that ancient like modern human society was affected with all forms of congenital anomalies. These included lethal abnormalities such as the spina bifida affecting one of the embalmed foetuses discovered in Tutankhamun's tomb in 1926. Other abnormalities reported from various mummies included clubfoot, cleft palate, and hydrocephalus. Tolerance towards malformed individuals was taught in the Instruction of Amenoemope dated to the end of the 2nd millennium BC: *Mock not the blind nor deride the dwarf nor block the cripple's path; don"t tease a man made ill by a god nor make outcry when he blunders.* Malformed individuals who survived were accepted in society and could advance themselves in the social hierarchy. In the ancient necropolis of Gaza and Saqqara, dwarves hailing from various professions – jewellers, animal handlers, fishermen, entertainers, nurses – are depicted in at least 50 tombs. At least 207 recorded representations of dwarfism have been recorded. There are in addition at least nine skeletons with dwarfism in the archaeological record.

Goldsmith artisan dwarfs on Tomb relief at Beni Hasan, 1980 B.C.

Some dwarfs reached the pinnacle of the social strata as evidenced by the VI Dynasty limestone-painted statute depicting the achondroplastic dwarf Seneb and his normal family who was honoured with a lavish tomb in a royal cemetery close to the pyramids. Seneb was the overseer of the palace dwarfs, chief of the royal wardrobe and priest of the funerary cults of Khufu. A fine statue in the Cairo Museum depicts him with his family, including his wife who was of normal stature, and two children. His wife was known to have been a lady of the court and a priestess.

Seneb and his family

Surgery

The Ancient Egyptians surgeons were apparently well versed with the principles of surgical treatment of traumatic injuries and other disorders. Much of the details of surgical practice can be gleaned from the *Edwin Smith Papyrus* [transcribed text can be seen at *http://www.reshafim.org.il/ad/egypt/timelines/topics/smithpapyrus.htm*]. This papyrus dates to 1550 BC and was found in the tomb of a physician. It is now housed in the New York Academy of Sciences.

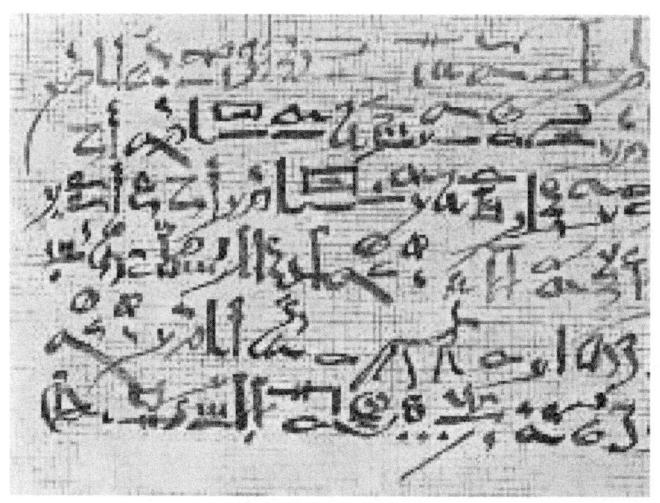

Edwin Smith Papyrus

The text in this papyrus gives an insight on the Egyptian doctor's approach to examining the patient leading to a diagnosis and subsequent treatment. The treatise is systematically organized in an arrangement of cases, which begin with injuries of the head and proceed downward through the body, like a modern treatise on anatomy. The treatment of these injuries is rational and chiefly surgical; there is resort to magic in only one case out of the forty-eight cases preserved. Each case is classified by one of three different verdicts: (1) favorable, (2) uncertain, or (3) unfavorable. The third verdict, expressed in the words, "an ailment not to be treated," is found in no other Egyptian medical treatise. The Edwin Smith Papyrus opens with eight texts concerning head wounds, followed by nineteen treatments of wounds to the face (forehead, eyebrows, nose, cheeks, temples, mouth, and chin), six descriptions of how to deal with injuries to throat and neck, five dealing with collar-bones and arms, and seven with chest complaints.

The papyrus suggests a highly sophisticated surgical practice which included the management of cranial injuries: *If thou examinest a man having a gaping wound in his head, penetrating the bone, smashing his skull, (and) rending open the brain of his skull, thou shouldst palpate his wound. Shouldst thou find that smash which is in his skull like those corrugations which form in molten copper, (and) something therein throbbing (and) fluttering under the fingers like the weak place of an infant's crown before it becomes whole- when it has happened there is no throbbing (and) fluttering under the fingers until the brain of his (the patient's) skull is rent open- (and) he discharges blood from both his nostrils, (and) he suffers with stiffness in his neck. Thou shouldst say concerning him: "An ailment not to be treated." Thou shouldst anoint that wound with grease. Thou shalt not bind it; thou shalt not apply two strips upon it: until thou knowest that he has reached a decisive point* [*Edwin Smith papyrus: case 6*].

Besides traumatic injuries, the surgeon also dealt with malignant tumours including breast cancer: *If thou examinest a man having tumors on his breast, (and) thou findest that swelling have spread over his breast; if thou puttest thy hand upon his breast upon these tumors, (and) thou findest them very cool, there being no fever at all therein when thy hand touches him ; they have no granulation , they form no fluid, they do not generate secretions of fluid, and they are bulging to thy hand . Thou shouldst say concerning him: "One having tumors. An ailment with which I will contend." There is no treatment. If thou findest tumors in any member of a man, thou shalt treat him according to these directions* [Edwin Smith papyrus: case 45]. Uterine cancer is mentioned in the Kahun and the Ebers texts: *Thou shalt say as to it: "What is the smell that thou emittest (lit. causest to be perceived)?" If she says to thee: "I am emitting the smell of roast meat," thou shalt say as to it, it is nemsu uteri. Thou shalt do for it (thus): fumigate her with every sort of roast meat, the smell of which she emits* [Kahun papyrus: case 2]. Another for one in whom there is eating on her uterus in whose vagina ulcers have appeared [Ebers papyrus]. At least 39 mummies suffering from cancer have been identified. The complication of tetanus or lockjaw was also identified and deemed untreatable: *If then, thou findest that the flesh of that man has developed fever from wound which is in the sutures of his skull, while that man has developed ty" from that wound, thou shouldst lay hand upon him. Shouldst find his countenance is clammy with sweat, the ligaments his neck are tense, his face ruddy, his teeth and his back, the odor of the chest of his head is like the bkn (urine) of sheep[7], his mouth is bound, (and) both his eyebrows are drawn, while his face is as if he wept. Thou shouldst say regarding him: "One having a gaping wound in his head penetrating to the bone, perforating the sutures of his skull; he has developed "ty", his mouth is bound, (and) he suffers with stiffness in his neck. An ailment not to be treated"* [*Edwin Smith papyrus: case 7*]. The Ebers Papyrus also describes the treatment for abscesses: *"Instructions for a swelling of pus .... A disease that I treat with knife-treatment. If anything remains in pocket, it recurs"* [*Ebers papyrus*]. The Edwin Smith Papyrus recommends the suturing of non-infected wounds with a needle and thread. Raw meat was applied on the first day, subsequently replaced by dressing of astringent herbs, honey and butter or bread.

*Men receiving massage therapy - **Tomb of the Physician, Saqqara***

Surgical procedures are also depicted in a number of tomb reliefs. The Tomb of Ankh-Mahor, known also as the Tomb of the Physician, at Saqqara has a relief showing two men receiving some form of treatment - manicure, massage or surgery – to their extremities. The accompanying text implores the physician: *Do not let it be painful*, to which the physician responds: *I do (it) so you will praise it, (O) king!*

Similarly, a relief depicted on the tomb of physician Sesi at Saqqara dated c.2400 BC depicts the performance of a circumcision of adolescents with the hieroglyphs saying: *The ointment is used to make it acceptable.* This has been interpreted as meaning that a local anaesthetic may have been used. Poppies *(Spn)* are occasionally mentioned in Egyptian medical literature, and the physicians must have had a pretty good idea of their properties. Female circumcision seems to have been practised occasionally: ... *I was circumcised, together with one hundred and twenty men, and one hundred and twenty women ...* [T*he Offering of Uha, c. 2400 BC*]. The care given to the injured in battle is depicted on a relief in the Great Temple of Abu Simbel.

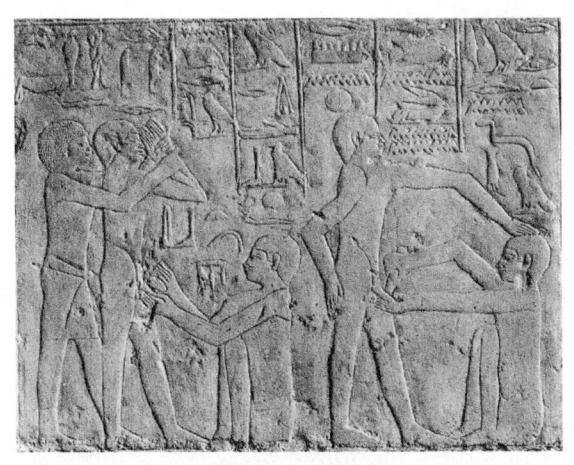

Circumcision

Treatment of battle injuries

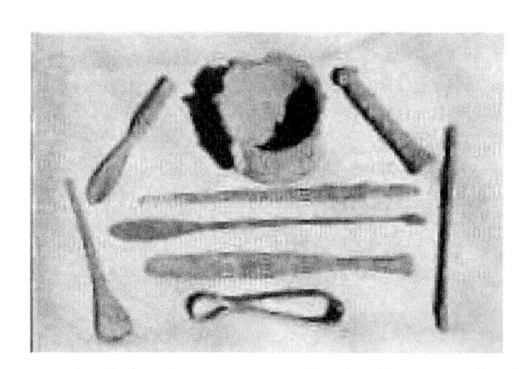

The Edwin Smith Papyrus contains a list of instruments, including lint, swabs, bandage, adhesive plaster (x-formed), support, surgical stitches and cauterization. The Cairo Museum has a collection of surgical instruments - including scalpels, scissors, copper needles, forceps, spoons, lancets, hooks, probes and pincers; some dating to the VI Dynasty discovered in the Tomb of Oar at Saqqara described as the senior physician of the royal court. The use of surgical instruments is also clearly mentioned in the Ebers Papyrus: *thou shalt perform an operation for it, the same being split with a knife and sized with a (?) forceps.*

A collection of 37 instruments are engraved on the wall in the temple of Sobek at Kom-Ombo (dated 2nd century BC). These include bone saws, suction cups, knives and scalpels, retractors, scales, lances, chisels and dental tools. Trepanation, while not mentioned in any of the medical papyri, but seems to have been performed occasionally using mallet and chisel since 14 skulls, some healed or partially healed, have been found. Limb amputations were also performed, the victims being assisted by the use of prosthesis. One mummy had three substitute teeth skillfully tied to the abutment teeth with fine gold wire.

Toe prosthesis

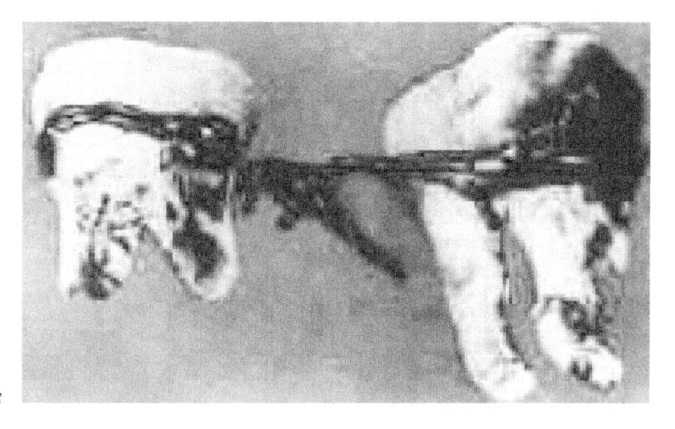

Dental prosthesis

Microscopy in the Pharaonic Period

It is generally accepted that the science of microscopy was invented by the Dutch draper Antoni van Leeuwenboek [1632-1723] who in his leisure made more than 400 microscopes. With his microscopes, he was able to make innumerable observations on a variety of micro-organisms and to describe the structure of various cells including the spermatozoa. His researches opened a new dimension to anatomical studies.

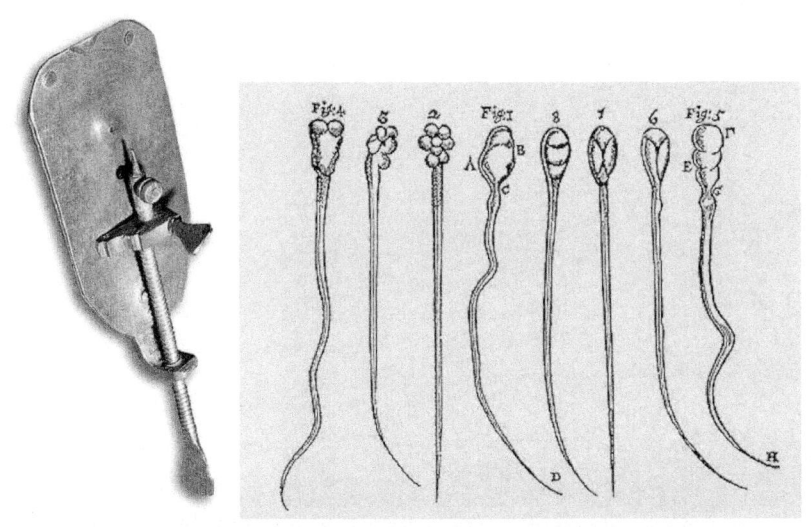

van Leeuwenboek microscope and speramatozoa diagram

Leeuwenboek's achievements may however have been only a re-discovery of previously known data. Pharaonic Egyptian culture had reached significant levels of expertise in the various sciences.

These advances may have also included knowledge about the histological structure of the spermatozoon. A temple frieze in the Barque Chamber at Luxor Temple shows the pharaoh collecting the "essence of life" from the fertility deity Amon-Ra, creator of the universe. The subsequent frieze shows the pharaoh with his double crown presenting his offering to the ithy-phallic deity wearing his plumed tiara. This latter frieze depicts the deity with an erect phallus exuding sperm. A close-up view of this frieze identifies a spermatozoon-like structure.

Temple frieze in the Barque Chamber at Luxor Temple

Known in the Egyptian language as *ipet resyt*, or "the southern harem", the temple was dedicated to the Theban Triad of Amon, Mut, and Chons and was, during the New Kingdom, the focus of the annual Opet Festival, in which a cult statue of Amun was paraded down the Nile from nearby Karnak Temple *(ipet-isut)* to stay there for a while, with his consort Mut, in a celebration of fertility. The Temple at Luxor was almost entirely built by Amenophis III, enlarged by Thutmosis III and completed by Ramses II during the XVIII-XIXth dynasties (14-15th millennium BC). The Sacred Barque Chamber, where the frieze is to be found, had doors made from acacia wood and inlaid with gold. Its present shape was actually given by Alexander the Great in the 4th century BC after he was recognised as the son of Amon-Ra by the oracle at Luxor. Alexander retained the original structure of Amenophis III, but removed the four columns and added a granite shrine.

The availability of magnification to the Egyptians is not surprising in the light of the discovery of a number of lenses from ancient times. One such crystal lens, discovered in Karanis, Egypt between 1924 and 1929, is kept in the Cairo Egyptian Museum. Dated to the 3rd century BC, the lens had been perfectly ground to give a magnification of about 1.5 times. Other period lenses are those discovered in Heluan, Egypt kept in the British Museum.

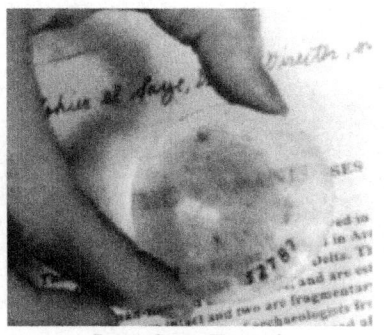

Lens from Karanis 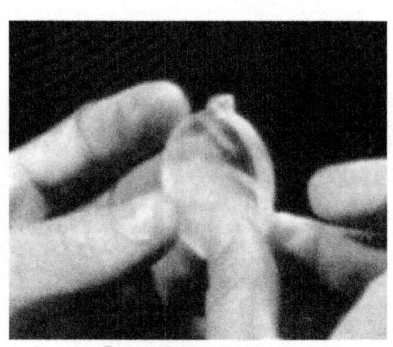 *Lens from Heluan*

The fine grinding of rock crystal to produce lenses in Egypt however dates significantly earlier to the IVth Dynasty (3rd millennium BC). This is evidenced by the numerous number ground rock-crystal eyes found in statutes dated to that period. These include the inlaid eyes found in the Nofret statute from Maydun and the seated scribe statute from Saqqara both in the Cairo Museum. These ground rock-crystal lenses have a convex surface and a flat base, except for a central concavity in the region of the pupil. These lenses confirm that the Egyptians had the necessary technology to manufacture optic-based instruments, including a high-resolution magnifying glass suitable for studying microscopic structures.

Nofret

Seated scribe

Medicine and therapeutics

While external disease or trauma was easily identifiable and related to a particular event, ancient populations often looked at internal disease as unexplainable and correlated with the influence of malicious spirits or deities. The Ancient Egyptians were no exception and often their medical culture developed mythological concepts to help protect them from internal disease. Mention has already been made of the recourse made by parturient women to the deities Bes and Taweret. Other deities in the Ancient Egyptian pantheon were attributed with protective and healing magical powers.

In the various Egyptian medical texts, Isis is shown to have held an important place in the pantheon of healing deities. Her legend is full of episodes of magic cures, and repeatedly she appears as the great magician whose counsel is the breath of life, whose sayings drive out sickness, and whose word gives life to him whose breath is failing. Horus, son of Isis and Osiris, was the falcon-headed sky god. The mythical story of his fight with Seth, established Horus as the god of the sun and god of life and of all good. During his battle against Seth, Horus has his eye gouged out. This was later restored by the deity Thoth. The eye of Horus (the Ugiat) remained a magical talisman for health throughout Egyptian history. The British Museum Medical Papyrus written at the end of the 18th Dynasty (circa 14th century BC) records how the Ugiat was invoked while applying a remedy to diseased eyes with the following charm recited four times. *"This Eye of Horus created by the spirits of Heliopolis, which Thoth has brought from Hermopolis – from the great hall in*

Heliopolis, - in Pe,- in Dep, sayest thou to it: "Welcome, thou splendid Eye of Horus, - thou content of the Eye of Horus – brought to drive out evil of the god, the evil of goddess, the demon, male and female, the dead, male and female, the enemy, male and female, who have insinuated themselves into the eyes of the sick under my fingers. – Protection, behind me protection, come protection!" Horus had also been stung by a deadly scorpion and was saved by the powerful spells of the gods. He thus was considered to have himself acquired special facilities to cure people bitten by venomous animals. The deity Ptah-Patecus, when depicted in his alternative form as a deformed dwarf with twisted legs, hands on hips and a huge head shaved except for the childish lock, played the role of protector against noxious animals and against all kinds of evil. The ibis-headed or dog-headed ape Thoth was considered a great physician and magician acting as physician to the god Horus. He was regarded as the god of magic, and was the arbiter between the gods and had the knowledge needed by the dead to pass safely through the underworld.. In the introduction to the Ebers Papyrus, it is stated that "*I* (Re, the sun god) *will save him from his enemies, and Thoth shall be his guide, he who lets writing speak and has composed books; he gives to the skilful, to the physicians who accompany him, skill to cure.*"

Recourse to the use of charms and invocations was also made as accompaniments to herbal medicine. It was expected that physical medicines, such as herbs assuaged pain; only the magical invocation affected the cure. Thus for example, the Ebers Papyrus describes several charms and invocations that were used to encourage healing. One is used before taking an herbal remedy as follows: "*Come Remedy! Come thou who expellest (evil) things in this my stomach and in these my limbs!"*; also the same text links the two perceived therapeutic options with the statement *"Magic is effective together with medicine. Medicine is effective together with magic"*. Other therapeutic options were used for various disease conditions, including massage: *"Examination of a woman aching in her legs and her calves after walking. You should say of it "it is discharges of the womb". You should treat it with a massage of her legs and calves with mud until she is well"* [Kahun Medical Papyrus]; as well as therapeutic herbs and foods.

Herbs played a major part in Egyptian medicine. Examples of prescriptions can be found in the Ebers Papyrus which mentions the use of opium, cannabis, myrrh, frankincense, fennel, cassia, senna, thyme, henna, juniper, aloe, linseed and castor oil. *"For the evacuation of the belly: Cow's milk, 1; .grains, 1; honey 1; mash, sift, cook; take in four portions……To remedy the bowels: Melilot (?), 1; dates, 1; cook in oil; anoint sick part……To refresh an aching head: Flour, 1; incense, 1; wood of wa, 1; waneb plant, 1; mint (?), 1; horn of a stag, 1; sycamore (?) seeds, 1; seeds of [(?)], 1; mason's plaster (?), 1; seeds of zart, 1; water, 1; mash, apply to the head……To renew bowel movements in a constipated child: An old book, boil in oil, apply half on the belly to re-establish evacuation."* [Ebers Papyrus]. Egyptians thought garlic and onions aided endurance, and consumed large quantities of them. Cloves of garlic have been found in Egyptian burial sites, including the tomb of Tutankhamen and in the sacred underground temple of the bulls at Saqqara. Leaves from many plants, such as willow, sycamore, acacia or the *ym*-tree, were used in poultices and the like. Tannic Acid derived from acacia nuts commonly helped heal burns. Tape worms, *the snakes in the belly*, were dealt with by an infusion of pomegranate root in water, which was strained and drunk. Animal products and minerals were also used as pharmacological agents. Honey and grease formed part of many wound treatments; mother's milk was occasionally given against viral diseases like the common cold; fresh meat laid on open wounds and sprains; and animal dung was thought to be effective at times. A cosmetics jar at the Cairo Museum bears the legend: "*Eye lotion to be dispersed, good for eyesight.*"

According to Herodotus there was a high degree of specialization among physicians: *The practice of medicine is very specialized among them. Each physician treats just one disease. The country is full of physicians, some treat the eye, some the teeth, some of what belongs to the abdomen, and others internal diseases.* [Herodotus, Histories 2,84]. Nothing certain is known about how physicians acquired their medical knowledge. It is probable that they were apprenticed to practicing healers. The field was mainly dominated by men, but was not restricted to women. An Old Kingdom female physician named Peseshet left a stele which recorded her positions of Overseer of Funerary Priestesses and of Overseer of Female Physicians.

Besides the medical conditions mentioned in the various medical papyri, evidence of disease states affecting the Ancient Egyptians is also furnished by the archaeological record.

Medical papyri

Much of the detailed information about the extent of the practice of medicine of the Ancient Egyptians comes from the rich source of textual material that has been found over the years. The main textual material comes from several Ancient Egyptian papyri which have a medical content. Most of these documents relate to diseases, remedies and the structure of the body as well as incantations and magic spells used as treatments in many cases. Most of these were discovered in the 19th and early 20th centuries, and no doubt these are only the tips of the iceberg. Many tracts must have been destroyed down through the years by natural phenomenon as well as by human intervention such as tomb robbers, military invasions and such like.

The ***Edwin Smith Papyrus*** is, without a doubt, one if the most important documents pertaining to medicine in the ancient Nile Valley. It was purchased by Edwin Smith in the 1862 after it was offered for sale by Mustafa Agha. It is now housed in the New York Academy of Sciences after being donated by his daughter in 1906. This papyrus is said to date from 1550 BC and was taken from the tomb of a physician. The papyrus includes 17 pages with 377 lines on the recto (front) and 5 pages with 92 lines on the verso (back) written with the same hand in a style of Middle Egyptian dating. It was translated by James Henry Breasted, director of the Oriental Institute at the University of Chicago, in 1930. This papyrus, in contrast to the other medical papyri, gives a unique view of Ancient Egyptian medicine since it illustrates the doctor's approach to patient examination to decide on a diagnosis and prognosis before giving the proposed treatment. It is mainly a work which deals with traumatic disorders and it is difficult to identify whether this was a typical general manual for the practitioner aimed at the treatment of daily injuries or whether it was a manual to manage injuries sustained in warfare. Unlike most of the other papyri this one is relatively free of magic and spells. [transcribed text can be seen at *http://www.reshafim.org.il/ad/egypt/timelines/topics/smithpapyrus.htm*]

This mainly traumatic surgery-oriented treatise is systematically organized in an arrangement of cases, which begin with injuries of the head and proceed downward through the body. The treatment of these injuries is rational and chiefly surgical; there is resort to magic in only one case out of the forty-eight cases preserved. Each case is classified by one of three different verdicts: (1) favorable, (2) uncertain, or (3) unfavorable. The third verdict, expressed in the words, "an ailment not to be treated," is found in no other Egyptian medical treatise. The Edwin Smith Papyrus opens with eight texts concerning head wounds, followed by nineteen treatments of wounds to the face (forehead, eyebrows, nose, cheeks, temples, mouth, and chin), six descriptions of how to deal with injuries to throat and neck, five dealing with collar-bones and arms, and seven with chest complaints.

The **Ebers Papyrus** was also purchased in Luxor by Edwin Smith in 1862. It was said to have come from a tomb on the West Bank, possibly the same tomb as the Edwin Smith Papyrus. It was said to have been found between the legs of a mummy in the Assassif district of the Theben necropolis. It was subsequently purchased by Georg Ebers in 1872 and eventually found its way to the University Library in Leipzig. In 1875, Ebers published a facsimile with an English-Latin vocabulary and introduction.

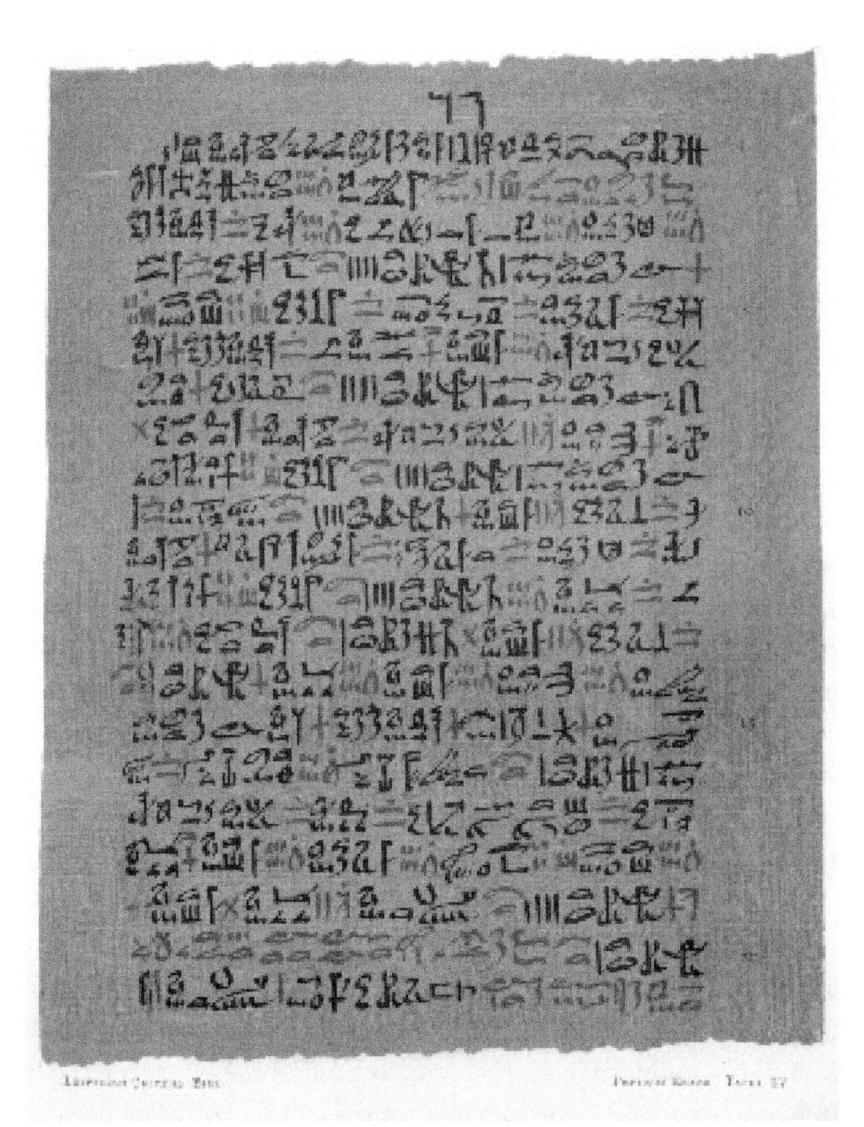

Ebers Papyrus

The papyrus is composed of 110 pages with some further text on the reverse side. It is dated by a passage on the verso to the 9th year of the reign of Amenhotep I (c. 1534 B.C.E.). However, Paragraph 856a states that: "the book of driving *wekhedu* from all the limbs of a man was found in writings under the two feet of Anubis in Letopolis and was brought to the majesty of the king of Upper and Lower Egypt *Den*." The reference to the Lower Egyptian *Den* is a historic anachronism which suggesting an origin closer to the First Dynasty (c. 3000 B.C.E.) The text is generally difficult to follow suggesting that it was a compilation from various sources with the scribe not entering remedies and ailments in the correct order. The structure of the papyrus is organized by paragraph, each of which are arranged into blocks addressing specific medical ailments. It deals with remedies of the skin, abdomen and other parts of the body; while the final part deals with surgical procedures, ulcers and tumours. [transcribed text at *http://www.reshafim.org.il/ad/egypt/timelines/topics/eberspapyrus.htm*]

Paragraphs 1-3 contain magical spells designed to protect from supernatural intervention on diagnosis and treatment. They are immediately followed by a large section on diseases of the stomach (*khet*), with a concentration on intestinal parasites in paragraphs 50-85. Skin diseases, with the remedies prescribed placed in the three categories of irritative, exfoliative, and ulcerative, are featured in paragraphs 90-95 and 104-118. Diseases of the anus, included in a section of the digestive section, are covered in paragraphs 132-164. Up to paragraph 187, the papyrus follows a relatively standardized format of listing prescriptions which are to relieve medical ailments. However, the diseases themselves are often more difficult to translate. Sometimes they take the form of recognizable symptoms such as an obstruction, but often may be a specific disease term such as *wekhedu* or *aaa*, the meaning of both of which remain quite obscure. Paragraphs 188-207 comprise "the book of the stomach," and show a marked change in style to something which is closer to the Edwin Smith Papyrus. Only paragraph 188 has a title, though all of the paragraphs include the phrase: "if you examine a man with a…," a characteristic which denotes its similarity to the Edwin Smith Papyrus. From this point, a declaration of the diagnosis, but no prognosis. After paragraph 207, the text reverts to its original style, with a short treatise on the heart (Paragraphs 208-241). Paragraphs 242-247 contains remedies which are reputed to have been made and used personally by various gods. Only in paragraph 247, contained within the above-mentioned section and relating to Isis" creation of a remedy for an illness in Ra's head, is a specific diagnosis mentioned. The following section continues with diseases of the head, but without reference to use of remedies by the gods. Paragraph 250 continues a famous passage concerning the treatment of migraines. The sequence is interrupted in paragraph 251 with the focus placed on a drug rather than an illness. Most likely an extract from pharmacopoeia, the paragraph begins: "Knowledge of what is made from *degem* (most likely a ricinous plant yielding a form of castor oil), as something found in ancient writings and as something useful to man." Paragraphs 261-283 are concerned with the regular flow of urine and are followed by remedies "to cause the heart to receive bread." Paragraphs 305-335 contain remedies for various forms of coughs as well as the *genew* disease. The remainder of the text goes on to discuss medical conditions concerning hair (paragraphs 437-476), traumatic injuries such as burns and flesh wounds (paragraphs 482-529), and diseases of the extremities such as toes, fingers, and legs. Paragraphs 627-696 are concerned with the relaxation or strengthening of the *metu*. The exact meaning of *metu* is confusing and could be alternatively translated as either mean hollow vessels or muscles tissue. The papyrus continues by featuring diseases of the tongue (paragraphs 697-704), dermatological conditions (paragraphs 708-721), dental conditions (paragraphs 739-750), diseases of the ear, nose, and throat (paragraphs 761-781), and gynecological conditions (paragraphs 783-839).

The **Kahun Papyrus** was discovered by Flinders Petrie in 1889 at the Fayum site of Lahun and was eventually deposited in the London University College. The papyrus is dated to this period by a note on the recto which states the date as being the 29th year of the reign of Amenenhat III (c. 1825 B.C.E.). The text was published in facsimile, with hieroglyphic transcription and translation into English, by Griffith in 1898. It is badly fragmented. The textual material is similar in style to the Edwin Smith Papyrus but deals mainly with gynaecological matters and other problems affecting women. The gynecological text can be divided into thirty-four paragraphs, of which the first seventeen have a common format. The first seventeen start with a title and are followed by a brief description of the symptoms, usually, though not always, having to do with the reproductive organs. The second section begins on the third page, and comprises eight paragraphs which, because of both the state of the extant copy and the language, are almost unintelligible. Despite this, there are several paragraphs that have a sufficiently clear level of language as well as being intact which can be understood. Paragraph 19 is concerned with the recognition of who will give birth; paragraph 20 is concerned with the fumigation procedure which causes conception to occur; and paragraphs 20-22 are concerned with contraception. Among those materials prescribed for contraception are crocodile dung, 45ml of honey, and sour milk. The third section (paragraphs 26-32) is concerned with the testing for pregnancy. Other methods include the placing of an onion bulb deep in the patient's flesh, with the positive outcome being determined by the odor appearing to the patients nose. The fourth and final section contains two paragraphs which do not fall into any of the previous categories. The first prescribes treatment for toothaches during pregnancy. The second describes what appears to be a fistula between bladder and vagina with incontinence of urine "in an irksome place." [transcribed text at *http://www.reshafim.org.il/ad/egypt/timelines/topics/kahunpapyrus.htm*]

The *Hearst Papyrus* was given in 1901 to the Expedition carried out by the University of California in Egypt by a peasant, in exchange for some waste soil he required as fertilizer. It is named after William Randolph Hearst, who funded much of the work of the expedition. The papyrus dates from the reign of Tuthmosis III in the 18th Dynasty in the first half of the second millennium BC. It consists of 18 pages with 260 paragraphs with hieratic Egyptian writing (a cursive form of hieroglyphic writing). Eighteen columns deal with medical prescriptions which concentrates on ailments of the urinary system, blood, hair and bites. The ailments for which cures are offered range from "a tooth which falls out" (Col. I, l. 7) and "remedy for treatment of the lung" (Col. IV, l. 8) to bites by human beings (Col. II, ll. 6–7), and pigs and hippopotami (Col. XVI, ll. 5–7). [*transcribed text can be seen at http://www.reshafim.org.il/ad/egypt/timelines/topics/hearstpapyrus.htm*]

The *Chester Beatty Papyri* was one of a series of 19 papyri donated to the British Museum by the millionaire industrialist Sir

Alfred Chester Beatty. These papyri were found in the workers village at Deir el-Medina in 1928. These papyri, together with many others now dispersed in various libraries was the private collection of the scribe Qen-her-khepeshef who lived in the 19th Dynasty and which were passed on down through his family until there were placed in a tomb. These papyri have undergone extensive reconstruction and translated into English by Gardiner in 1935. Their content comprises many magical incantations against headache; but there is much space given over to vague rectal ailments with various remedies and incantations.

The **Berlin Papyrus** was acquired by Giuseppe Passalacqua in Sakkara and was sold on to Friedrich Wilhelm IV of Prussia with other objects in 1827 for the Berlin Museum. It was originally translated into German by Wreszinski in 1909. The style suggests a 19th Dynasty origin. It is made up of 24 pages - 21 verso and 3 retro – and its content is similar to the Ebers papyrus.

The **London Medical Papyrus** was passed on to the British Museum in 1860 having been in the possession of the Royal Institute of London prior to that. Its style dates it to the reign of Tutankhamun. It is comprised of 19 pages but is in very poor condition. It concentrates mostly on magical spells.

The **Ramesseum Papyri** was discovered in the great temple of the Ramesseum. The group of 17 papyri are believed to date to the 13th Dynasty (Early Second Intermediate Period). The main medical content is concentrated in Parts III, IV and V, all written in vertical columns. These sections discuss diseases of the eyes, gynaecological conditions, diseases affecting children, and those affecting muscles and tendons.

The ***Carlsberg Papyrus*** is the property of the Carlsberg Foundation and is housed in the Egyptological Institute of the University of Copenhagen. Its style dates it to the 19th/20th Dynasties. It deals mainly with eye disease and pregnancy; and bears similarities to the Kahun and Berlin papyri.

The ***Brooklyn Papyrus*** is housed in the Brooklyn Museum. The style relates this to the Ebers Papyrus and has been dated to the 30th Dynasty or Early Ptolemic Period. It discusses various remedies to drive out the poison from snakes, scorpions and tarantulas.

The above-mentioned contemporary medical texts have furnished an extensive insight into the medical practice and knowledge of the Ancient Egyptians. Other textual information has also been gleaned from inscribed text found on sculptured reliefs and on pieces of pottery and ostraca, particularly from those dating from the Amarna Period to the time of Roman occupation. An example of such fragmentary textual sources is a little pink pot bears the following hieratic inscription:

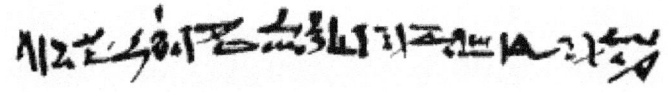

which, read from right to left, means: *Saw dust, acacia leaves, galena, goose fat. Bandage with it.*

Further information may be obtained by studying other contemporary texts from the region. The Torah and other rabbinical texts are another such source of medical-related concepts especially as this relates to reproductive health.

Reproductive issues in the Torah

The Torah [Hebrew: תּוֹרָה], meaning instruction, is a compendium of Judaism's founding legal and ethical religious texts written during the Babylonian exile circa 600 BCE and completed during the Persian period circa 400 BCE. The Torah consists of the first five books of the Jewish biblical canon and has been adopted by Christianity being incorporated as part of the Old Testament. Known as the Pentateuch, the books include: the Bereshit – Genesis; Shemot – Exodus; Vayikra – Leviticus; Bamidbar – Numbers; and Devarim – Deuteronomy. The Torah is written in the form of a narrative starting with the creation of the world, the early history of the people of Israel, their Egyptian sojourn, the Egyptian exodus and the giving of the law at Mount Sinai, and ending with the death of Moses just before the people of Israel reach the promised land. The Torah thus recounts earlier historical folktales of the Hebrew [or Khabiru] population predating the Iron Age [before 1400 BCE]. The Khabiru moved in the Palestinian region as mercenaries, casual labourers or brigands from the desert margin to the east. They have often been equated with the Hebrew tribe returning through the desert from their sojourn in Egypt.[1]

The books are however not simply a historical narrative, but contain specific teachings related to religious obligations and civil laws of this community. Supplemented by the Jewish Apocrypha and later books of the Old Testament together with archaeological

---

[1] Trump DH. The Prehistory of the Mediterranean. Penguin Books, Middlesex, U.K., 1981; Pritchard J.B. (editor). Ancient Near Eastern Texts relating to the Old Testament. Princeton University Press, New Jersey, 1950.

remains in the region, these writings have a wealth of reflections that deal with the various human lifecycles as perceived by human society at the time. These cycles include Birth-Sexuality-Death, Puberty-Fertility-Menopause, and Conception-Pregnancy-Parturition. This corpus thus reflects on fertility and its control, on concepts relating to aetiology of miscarriages and malformations, and further relate the contemporary management of labour and delivery besides describing a number of abnormal obstetric cases. These concepts can be compared and contrasted with the contemporary archaeological records and medical papyri found in the adjoining land of Egypt. The Ancient Egyptians with their belief in the afterlife left detailed representations of their way of life in the various contemporary inscriptions and pictograms left in their tombs and temples. Gynaecological problems and their management in Ancient Egypt are mainly documented in the *Kahun Gynaecological Papyrus*. The Kahun Papyrus, housed in the University College London, is dated to this period by a note on the recto which states the date as being the 29th year of the reign of Amenenhat III (c. 1825 B.C.E.).[2]

Fertility and Infertility: Fertility was a central theme of many Neolithic cultures prevalent around the Mediterranean basin. It served also as the basis of the extended family's economy. Fertility was particularly directed towards the agricultural and husbandry gifts of the so-called fertility deity that enable the survival of the community. In the Semitic mythology, the Semitic mother goddess

---

[2] Griffith FL. The Petrie Papyri: Hieratic Papyri from Kahun and Gurob - Principally of the Middle Kingdom. Quaritch, London, U.K., 1898. [See http://archive.org/details/hieraticpapyrifr00grifuoft. For translated text by Quirke S. see: http://www.digitalegypt.ucl.ac.uk/med/birthpapyrus.html].

refers to Asherah (Hebrew: אֲשֵׁרָה). It appears the Hebrews continued to worship Asherah even after their supposed adoption of monotheism, and "the worship of Baal and Asherah persisted among the Israelites for over seven centuries, from the period after the conquest and settlement of Canaan, which most biblical scholars place at around 1400 BC, to the time of the destruction of Jerusalem by Nebuchadnezzar and the exile of the Israelites in Babylon in the 6th century BC".[3] The abrogation of the cult of Asherah was strongly advocated in the Torah books. *Exodus* 34:13 states: *"But ye shall destroy their altars, break their images, and cut down their groves"* [referring to the Asherah poles]; while *Deuteronomy* 16:21-22 states *"Thou shalt not plant thee a grove* [Asherah pole] *of any trees near unto the altar of the LORD thy God, which thou shalt make thee. Neither shalt thou set thee up any image; which the LORD thy God hateth."* The term *"groves"* in the King James Version refers to the Asherah pole, a sacred tree or pole that stood near the Canaanite religious locations to honour Asherah. Further reference to the cult of Asherah [or Ashtoreth] within Hebrew culture is made in later books of the Old Testament. King Manasseh [reign circa 687 – 643 BCE] is reported to have placed an Asherah pole in the Jewish Holy Temple at Jerusalem. *2 Kings* 21:7 states that *"he [Manasseh] set a graven image of the grove that he had made in the house, of which the LORD said to David, and to Solomon his son, In this house, and in Jerusalem, which I have chosen out of all tribes of Israel, will I put my name forever."* These were subsequently destroyed and removed by King Josiah [reign circa 641–609 BCE] with *2 Kings* 23:6 stating that *"he [Josiah] brought out the grove from the house of the LORD, without Jerusalem, unto the brook Kidron, and burned*

---

[3] James N. The origins and role of same-sex relations in human societies. McFarland & Company, Jefferson, NC, 2008.

it at the brook Kidron, and stamped it small to powder, and cast the powder thereof upon the graves of the children of the people". Asherah was considered to be the deity responsibility for fertility and infertile Hebrew women may have resorted to this deity to overcome their problem. The previously infertile Rachel is known to have taken the pagan household deity images from her father's house sited in Haran and *"put them in the camel's furniture, and sat upon them. And Laban searched all the tent, but found them not"* [Genesis 31:35]. Haran is almost universally identified with Harran, an Assyrian city in Upper Mesopotamia whose ruins lie within present-day Turkey. The Assyrians followed the polytheistic Assyro-Babylonian religion. Their pantheon included Ishtar, equated with the Ugarit Asherah, who was the goddess of fertility, war, love, and sex.[4]

High fertility was thus strongly desired being viewed as an enrichment of the extended family group in both nomadic and farming societies. The birth of a child, particularly a son, was considered to be a gift from Yahweh reflecting his benevolence on the woman and family or simply in compensation. *"And God blessed them, and God said unto them, Be fruitful, and multiply, and replenish the earth, and subdue it: and have dominion over the fish of the sea, and over the fowl of the air, and over every living thing that moveth upon the earth".* [Genesis 1:28] *"And Adam knew Eve his wife; and she conceived, and bare Cain, and said, I have gotten a man from the LORD."* [Genesis 4:1] *"And when the LORD saw that Leah was hated, he opened her womb..."*. [Genesis 29:31] Fertile women were honoured while the barren were to be pitted. Thus *"And when Rachel saw that she bare Jacob no children, Rachel envied her*

---

[4] Sykes E. Who's Who in non-Classic Mythology. University Press, Oxford, U.K.,1993.

sister; and said unto Jacob, Give me children, or else I die." [Genesis 30:1]. The Kahun Papyrus gives a number of features one should look for to assess whether the woman is fertile or infertile. These varied methods range from a simple examination of the breasts to placing an onion bulb in the vagina overnight and identifying the odour in the patient's nose the next day. One could also determine the number of children she would bear by assessing the number of times the woman vomits after being made to sit on the ground smeared with dregs of beer and given fruit [? dates].[5]

Very grand multiparity was however not the norm. The majority of families mentioned in the Torah had six to seven children [Japheth – 7 children; Cush – 6 children; Mizraim – 7 children; Keturah – 6 children; Milcah – 7 children; Eliphae – 7 children; Leah – 6 children]. Others had less. Only Joktun and Ismael had 13 and 14 children respectively, though the text does not define whether these were from one spouse or more. Fertility throughout a woman's reproductive life, without the facility of contraception, would have been controlled by the prolonged lactation period and delayed infant weaning common in earlier practices even though wet-nursing was apparently practiced especially in the higher social strata. Thus, when the Pharaoh's daughter discovered Moses in the basket among the reeds, the first thought was of finding a wet nurse to care for the child. *"Then said his sister to Pharaoh's daughter, Shall I go and call to thee a nurse of the Hebrew women, that she may nurse the child for thee?"* [Exodus 2:7] The wet nurse became an important feature of the child's eventual life accompanying the child in

---

[5] Griffith FL, 1898, *op. cit.*

adulthood so that "they sent away Rebekah their sister, and her nurse, and Abraham's servant, and his men". [Genesis 24:59]

Active forms of contraception were not generally desired or the norm. However coitus interruptus was practiced by Onan to deprive his sister-in-law Tamar the opportunity to continue his dead brother's family line, an obligation placed upon him by his father Judah. Onan was punished for his actions. Thus *"Judah said unto Onan, Go in unto thy brother's wife, and marry her, and raise up seed to thy brother. And Onan knew that the seed should not be his; and it came to pass, when he went in unto his brother's wife, that he spilled it on the ground, lest that he should give seed to his brother. And the thing which he did displeased the LORD: wherefore he slew him also."* [Genesis 38:8-10] The importance of maintaining and propagating the family line occasionally led to drastic measures to achieve impregnation by the head of the family. Tamar eventually resorted to subterfuge to achieve a pregnancy. Disguising herself as a prostitute, she enticed her father-in-law to impregnate her to become pregnant with twins. [Genesis 38:15-27] Similarly Lot's daughters resorted to incest getting themselves impregnated by their father after getting him drunk to *"preserve seed of our father"*. [Genesis 19:32] Both daughters thus became pregnant by their father. The use of a hand-maid or slave-girl as a form of surrogacy was also resorted to. In the light of her apparent infertility, Rachel offered her spouse Jacob her maid Bilhah to serve as an alternative surrogate spouse to carry a child stating *"Behold my maid Bilhah, go in unto her; and she shall bear upon my knees that I may also have children by her"*. [Genesis 30:3] Similarly Sarah offered the Egyptian slave girl Hagar for the same purpose telling Abram *"Behold now, the LORD hath restrained me from bearing: I pray thee, go in unto my maid; it may be that I may obtain children by her. And Abram hearkened to the voice of Sarai"*. [Genesis 16:1-2]

Other alternative means to achieve contraception in the 2nd millennium BCE are described in the Kahun Papyrus. These include resorting to the use of a mixture of crocodile dung chopped over HsA and awyt-liquid; or sprinkling honey on the womb upon a bed of natron; or sprinkling the womb with HsA and awyt-liquid.[6] Other forms of contraception included male sterilization since eunuchs were apparently a feature of Jewish society described in later Old Testament books – *"Neither let the son of the stranger, that hath joined himself to the LORD, speak, saying, The LORD hath utterly separated me from his people: neither let the eunuch say, Behold, I am a dry tree. For thus saith the LORD unto the eunuchs that keep my sabbaths, and choose the things that please me, and take hold of my covenant; Even unto them will I give in mine house and within my walls a place and a name better than of sons and of daughters: I will give them an everlasting name, that shall not be cut off"*. [Isaiah 56:3-5]

Infertility was considered a punishment from Yahweh who closed the wombs of women considered sterile. Thus, Jacob's rejoinder to his sterile wife's plea to impregnate her was *"Am I in Yahweh's stead, who hath withheld from thee the fruit of the womb?"* [Genesis 30:2] Rachel possibly had an obesity-related subfertility since we are told that *"Leah was tender eyed; but Rachel was beautiful and well favoured"*. [Genesis 29:17] In Semitic mentality, *"well favoured"* could very well have referred to generously endowed pelvic proportions as depicted in the pagan deity Asherah.

---

[6] Griffith FL, 1898, *ibid.*

Household infertility was also Yahweh's punishment to Abimelech who had unknowingly taken Abraham's spouse Sarah to his harem. In this episode, Yahweh is said to have closed the wombs of all women in Abimelech's household – or was this a case of self-limiting male infertility? Being the result of a misdemeanor, the curse of infertility was removed after *"Abraham prayed unto Yahweh: and Yahweh healed Abimelech, and his wife, and his maidservants; and they bore children. For the LORD had fast closed up all the wombs of the house of Abimelech, because of Sarah Abraham's wife"*. [Genesis 20:17-18] Sarah herself was infertile, though her infertility was attributed to age-related cessation of menses since the Genesis 18:11 reports that *"Now Abraham and Sarah were old and well stricken in age; and it ceased to be with Sarah after the manner of women"*.

Phytotherapy in the form on *duda"im* was also resorted to by Rachel in the management of her infertility. *"And Reuben went in the days of wheat harvest, and found duda"im in the field, and brought them unto his mother Leah. Then Rachel said to Leah, Give me, I pray thee, of thy son's duda"im. And she said unto her, Is it a small matter that thou hast taken my husband? and wouldest thou take away my son's duda"im also? And Rachel said, Therefore he shall lie with thee to night for thy son's duda"im"*. [Genesis 30:14-15] It is difficult to botanically identify the *duda"im*, which seemingly is available at the time of the harvest. Most biblical commentators identify the plant as the mandrake based on the fact that the word *duda"im* has the same numerical value as *ke"adam* meaning "like man". The mandrake root resembles the human form with head, hands and feet. Because of the human shape of its root, mandrake was universally associated with fertility.[7] Rachel eventually conceived and normally delivered a healthy normal male infant, the conception attributed as a gift from God. *"And Yahweh remembered Rachel, and Yahweh hearkened to her, and opened her womb. And she conceived, and bare a son; and said, Yahweh hath taken away my reproach: And she called his name Joseph; and said, The LORD shall add to me another son"*. [Genesis 30:22-24] Her second pregnancy conceived spontaneously was to terminate in a complicated labour and delivery resulting in her death. The Kahun papyrus further gives a recipe to assist pregnancy: *after ceases the return .... pound, grind fine, [strain] in cloth on gruel auyt, pour mehuyu .... Incense, fresh fat, dates, sweet beer, put inside a rack (of wood) in the flame; thou shalt fumigate .... as a sweetener of the mouth*.[8]

A diagnosis of pregnancy was made on the ability of pregnant urine to germinate cereals: *"Another test for woman who will bear or a woman who will not bear. Wheat and spelt: let the woman water them daily with her urine like dates and like sh"at seeds in two bags. If they both grow, she will bear; if the wheat grows, it will be a boy; if the spelt grows, it will be a girl. If neither grows, she will not bear"*. Investigations to assess whether there is any truth in this diagnostic test have suggested that it may actually be useful to detect pregnancy but not identify the foetal gender.[9]

---

[7] Rosner F. Pharmacology and dietetics in the Bible and the Talmund. In. Jacob I, Jacob W, editors. The Healing Past – Pharmaceutical in the Biblical and Rabbinic World. E.J. Brill, Leiden, Netherlands, 1993.

[8] Griffith FL, 1898, *op. cit.*

[9] Ghalioungui P, Khalil SH, AmmarAR. On an Ancient Egyptian method of diagnosing pregnancy and determining foetal sex. Medical History 1963; 7(3):241–246

Pregnancy and childbirth: Pregnancy is fraught with a number of complications during the antenatal period and the during the delivery process. One cause for miscarriages or early pregnancy interruption mentioned in the Torah is physical trauma – *"If men strive, and hurt a woman with child, so that her fruit depart from her, and yet no mischief follow: he shall be surely punished, according as the woman's husband will lay upon him; and he shall pay as the judges determine. And if any mischief follow, then thou shalt give life for life, Eye for eye, tooth for tooth, hand for hand, foot for foot, Burning for burning, wound for wound, stripe for stripe"*. [Exodus 21:22-25] The Ebers Papyrus gives an abortive remedy, using a ground mixture of the acanthus fruit, onion and dates pulverized in a vessel containing honey. The mixture is sprinkled on a cloth and applied to the vulva [or inserted into the vagina]. The Ebers Papyrus was said to have been found in the Assassif district of the Theben necropolis. It is dated by a passage on the verso to the 9th year of the reign of Amenhotep I (c. 1534 B.C.E.).[10]

Foetal development was seen as dependent on the male element with the womb acting a nourishing molding receptacle for the child. This is clearly described in the Wisdom of Solomon, a later text of the Old Testament: *"I myself also am a mortal man, like to all, and the offspring of him that was first made of the earth, And in my mother's womb was fashioned to be flesh in the time of ten months, being compacted in blood, of the seed of man, and the pleasure that came with sleep. And when I was born, I drew in the common air, and fell upon the earth, which is of like nature, and the first voice*

---

[10] Joachim H. Papyros Ebers. Das älteste buch über heilkunde. G. Reimer, Berlin, 1860. [English translated text available in: Bryan CP. The Papyrus Ebers. Geoffrey Bles, London, U.K., 1930].

which I uttered was crying, as all others do. I was nursed in swaddling clothes, and that with cares. For there is no king that had any other beginning of birth. For all men have one entrance into life, and the like going out". [Wisdom of Solomon 7:1-6] The mentioned ten months refer to the ten lunar months required for foetal development.

Foetal development within the maternal womb was believed in the Torah to affected by visual impressions – *"And Jacob took him rods of green poplar, and of the hazel and chestnut tree; and pilled white strakes in them, and made the white appear which was in the rods. And he set the rods which he had pilled before the flocks in the gutters in the watering troughs when the flocks came to drink, that they should conceive when they came to drink. And the flocks conceived before the rods, and brought forth cattle ringstraked, speckled, and spotted"*. [Genesis 30:37-39] There can be no doubt that ancient like modern human society was affected with all forms of congenital anomalies. These included lethal abnormalities such as the spina bifida affecting one of the embalmed foetuses discovered in Tutankhamen's tomb in 1926. Other abnormalities reported from various mummies included clubfoot, cleft palate, and hydrocephalus.[11]

Tolerance towards malformed individuals was taught in the Instruction of Amenemope dated to the end of the 2nd millennium BC: *"Do not laugh at a blind man nor scorn a dwarf nor spoil the plan of a lame man. Do not scorn a man who is the hand of god nor be fierce of countenance towards him when he has erred"*. [Teaching

---

[11] Harrison RG, Connolly RC, Ahmed S, Abdalla AB, El Ghawby M, A mummified foetus from the Tomb of Tutankhamen. Antiquity 1979; 53:19-21

of Amenemope, xxiv, 9-12][12] Malformed individuals who survived were accepted in society and could advance themselves in the social hierarchy. A relief in the tomb of Mereruka at Saqqara [ca.2330 BCE] depicts dwarves involved in metallurgical works. At least another 200 depictions of dwarves are found in other tombs at Gaza and Saqqara.[13] Some dwarfs reached the pinnacle of the social strata as evidenced by the VI Dynasty limestone-painted statute depicting the achondroplastic dwarf Seneb and his normal family who was honoured with a lavish tomb in a royal cemetery close to the pyramids. Seneb was the overseer of the palace dwarfs, chief of the royal wardrobe and priest of the funerary cults of Khufu. A fine statue in the Cairo Museum depicts him with his family, including his wife who was of normal stature, and two children. His wife was known to have been a lady of the court and a priestess.[14]

The antenatal period could be a very uncomfortable one especially when the pregnancy was a twin gestation – *"..Rebekah his wife conceived. And the children struggled together within her; and she said, If it be so, why am I thus?"* [Genesis 25:22-23] Twin pregnancies could be monozygotic or dizygotic. The twin brothers Pharez and Zarah born to Tamar appear to have been monozygotic sharing the same amniotic cavity. During the delivery, Zarah had a prolapsed arm that was pulled back into the uterus allowing the eventual birth of his twin. – *"And it came to pass in the time of her travail, that, behold, twins were in her womb. And it came to pass, when she travailed, that the one put out his hand: and the midwife*

---

[12] Teaching of Amenemope, xxiv, 9-12. In: John Ruffle, The teaching of Amenemope and its connection with the Book of Proverbs, Tyndate Bulletin, 1977, 28: 29-68
[13] Schulz R, Seidel M. Egypt – The World of the Pharaohs. Konemann, Germany, 2004
[14] Carpiceci AC, Art and history of Egypt: 5000 years of civilization. Bonechi, Florence, 2000

took and bound upon his hand a scarlet thread, saying, This came out first, And it came to pass, as he drew back his hand, that, behold, his brother came out: and she said, How hast thou broken forth? this breach be upon thee: therefore his name was called Pharez. And afterward came out his brother, that had the scarlet thread upon his hand: and his name was called Zarah". [Genesis 38:27-30] The twin brothers Esau and Jacob were on the other hand dizygotic and non-identical twins – *"And Jacob said to Rebekah his mother, "And Jacob said to Rebekah his mother, Behold, Esau my brother is a hairy man, and I am a smooth man".* [Genesis 27:11] The birth of the non-identical twin birth of Esau and Jacob to Rebekah, wife of Isaac is described in Genesis 25:24-26 – *"And when her days to be delivered were fulfilled, behold, there were twins in her womb. And the first came out red, all over like an hairy garment; and they called his name Esau. And after that came his brother out, and his hand took hold on Esau's heel; and his name was called Jacob: and Isaac was threescore years old when she bare them".*

Parturition as described in the Torah was managed by midwives or traditional birth attendants who used birthing stools to achieve delivery. *"Then the king of Egypt said to the Hebrew midwives, one of whom was named Shiph"rah and the other Pu"ah, "When you serve as midwife to the Hebrew women, and see them upon the birthstool, if it is a son, you shall kill him; but if it is a daughter, she shall live." But the midwives feared Yahweh, and did not do as the king of Egypt commanded them, but let the male children live".* [Exodus 1:15-17]

Birthing stools were widespread tools throughout the eastern Mediterranean with archaeological evidence for their use being described in Egypt – e.g. relief at the Temple of Hathor at Dendera. An alternative method of delivery may have been with the woman sitting on her hunches with legs raised on bricks/stones with an assistant supporting the back. This may have the meaning of Rachel's comment relating to her maid's delivery when she states that *"... she may bear upon my knees...."*. [Genesis 30:3]

Assisted Birth with mother held by attendant, Cyprus

Birthing bricks have been excavated from the archaeological site at Abydos in Egypt, while a Ptolemiac Period statuette depicting a parturient woman sitting on her haunches with legs raised has been excavated from Egypt. Alternative birthing positions in noted in Egyptian archaeology appears to be the squatting position as evident in the relief showing the parturient woman at Sobek Temple at Kom Ombo. Egyptian women appear to have withdrawn to birth huts outside the house for the birth and for a ritual purification period of at least two weeks. These birth huts may have been the precursors of the birth houses or *mammisi* annexed to Ptolemaic period temples, e.g. at Dendera, Edfu and Philae. These *mammisi* may have also been extant in temples from the New Kingdom such as the temples of Mut at Karnak, the temple of Luxor, and Deir el-Bahari. These birth houses served to request divine help by pregnant women rather than being a birthing place. Egyptian deities commonly associated with the protection of mother and child such as Bes and Taueret were often depicted in these houses.[15] Bes was depicted as a dwarf with ugly features. The appearance was meant to frighten off any spirits that might be harmful to the child. Taueret was depicted with the head of a hippopotamus, the legs and arms of a lion, the tail of a crocodile, human breasts, and a swollen belly. She was often depicted holding the Sa amulet symbolizing protection.[16]

The birthing process was reported to be generally smooth and quick in Hebrew women preceding the arrival of the midwife so that *"The midwives said to Pharaoh, "Because the Hebrew women are not like the Egyptian women; for they are vigorous and are delivered before the midwife comes to them."* [Exodus 1:19] Labour pains were assumed to be a punishment from Yahweh based on the comment that *"To the woman he said, "I will greatly multiply your pain in childbearing; in pain you shall bring forth children".* [Genesis 3:16] While the midwives' comments to the Pharaoh suggest a generally smooth delivery, this was not always the case. The Jewish Apocrypha test states that *"Then were the entrances of this world made narrow, full of sorrow and travail: they are but few and evil,*

---

[15] Kockelmann H. Mammisi - Birth House. In: Wendrich W. (editor). UCLA Encyclopedia of Egyptology. UCLA, Los Angeles, 2011. [see http://digital2.library.ucla.edu/viewItem.do?ark=21198/zz0026wfgr]

[16] Sykes E., 1993, *op. cit.*

full of perils, and very painful". [4 Esedra 7:12][17] A number of complicated deliveries are described in the Torah. The worst obstetric case scenario was the birth of Benjamin to Rachel. This was the second pregnancy of Rachel, having previously given birth without mishap to Joseph. This pregnancy was apparently spontaneous probably conceived during the undertaking an arduous journal since she was apparently menstruation in the early phase of the journey since on encountering her father, Rachel 'said to her father, *"Let it not displease my lord that I cannot rise up before thee; for the custom of women is upon me"*. [Genesis 31:35] The *"custom of women"* generally refers to menstruation when used in the Torah books, it could also possibly refer to pregnancy in this instance. During the journey, she started labour, possibly prematurely. The labour was difficult and prolonged. The foetus was presenting in the breech enabling the midwife to determine the gender prior to its delivery. Rachel passed away soon after the delivery of her son possibly as a result of postpartum haemorrhage resulting from uterine atonia following the prolonged labour. [Genesis 35:18-19] Uterine inertia from atonia is further mentioned in a later book of the Old Testament with the statement *"....for the children are come to the birth, and there is not strength to bring forth"*. [2 Kings 19:3] Other described intrapartum problems described in the Torah is the case of prolapsed arm of the presumably monoamniotic second twin with spontaneous resolution and delivery mentioned earlier. The prognostic signs of survival of the newborn were detailed by the Ebers Papyrus: *"Another way of knowing about a child the day he is born: If he says ni, it will live. If he says ba, it will die."* Another way

---

[17] '4 Esedra 7:12. See Jerome. Vulgate Bible. Bible Foundation and On-Line Book Initiative. [See ftp.std.com/obi/Religion/Vulgate].

of knowing: *"If it let a loud lamentation be heard, it will die. If it looks down its face it will thereupon die."*[18]

The Torah fails to detail management options in cases of obstructed labour. According to the Ebers papyrus labours could be aided by applying peppermint to the buttocks, or pouring crushed pot of a new hennu vessel in warm oil to the genitals. Another recipe included plastering a mixture of sea salt, wheat grain and female reed onto the abdomen. A mixture of salt and honey taken orally was also supposed to help.[19] The Hebrew Talmud refers to resorting to post-mortem Caesarean section when discussing whether undertaking to perform the procedure during the Sabbath was permissible – *"Only cutting flesh? Rabbah said: It is necessary [to permit the] fetching of the knife by way of a public thoroughfare? But what is he informing us? That in case of doubt one may desecrate the Sabbath! ..... Here where it [the embryo] did not have such original presumption of life, one might say no [desecration of the Sabbath shall be permitted], therefore we are informed [that it is]"* [Talmud – Arachin 7b:1-3].[20] Intra-uterine foetal destruction to manage obstructed labour was considered an acceptable option – *"If a woman has difficulty in childbirth, we cut up the offspring in her womb and remove it limb by limb, because her life comes before its life. If most of it [the child] has come out, we do not touch it, because we do not push aside one life for another"* [Talmud - Ohalot 7:6].[21] Prolonged labour could have dire consequences leading to a maternal death as

---

[18] Joachim H., 1860, *op. cit.*
[19] Joachim H., 1860, *ibid.*
[20] Talmud – Arachin 7b:1-3. In: Arachin – Translated into English with notes. The Soncino Babylonian Talmund Folios 2a-34a [see http://halakhah.com/rst/kodoshim/45%20-%20Arachin.pdf].
[21] Talmud - Ohalot 7:6 [see http://halakhah.com/pdf/taharoth/Oholoth.pdf].

in the case of Rachel or maternal anatomical damage. The mummy of Pharaoh's Queen Henhenit dated circa 2050 BCE discovered in Thebes was found to have a vesicovaginal fistula. The mummy had an abnormally shaped pelvis with a reduced transverse diameter and a high sacral promontory. Obstructed labour probably caused her death as the baby was likely to have been delivered with force, causing the bladder tear.[22]

Management of the Puerperium: The Hebrews had very strict hygienic laws that detailed the period of time the woman was considered unclean because of her lochial discharge. The duration depended on the gender of the child lasting 40 days after the birth of a son and 80 days after the birth of a daughter – *"And the Lord spake unto Moses, saying, Speak unto the children of Israel, saying, If a woman have conceived seed, and born a man child: then she shall be unclean seven days; according to the days of the separation for her infirmity shall she be unclean. And in the eighth day the flesh of his foreskin shall be circumcised. And she shall then continue in the blood of her purifying three and thirty days; she shall touch no hallowed thing, nor come into the sanctuary, until the days of her purifying be fulfilled. But if she bore a maid child, then she shall be unclean two weeks, as in her separation: and she shall continue in the blood of her purifying threescore and six days"* [Leviticus 12:1-7]. In addition, *"if a woman have an issue of her blood many days out of the time of her separation, or if it run beyond the time of her separation; all the days of the issue of her uncleanness shall be as the days of her separation: she shall be unclean. Every bed whereon she lieth all the days of her issue shall be unto her as the bed of her*

---

[22] Derry DE. Note on five pelvises of women of the eleventh dynasty in Egypt. Journal of Obstetrics and Gynaecology in the British Empire 1935; 42: 490.

separation: and whatsoever she sitteth upon shall be unclean, as the uncleanness of her separation. And whosoever toucheth those things shall be unclean, and shall wash his clothes, and bathe himself in water, and be unclean until the evening" [Leviticus 15:25-27].

Infants were breastfed up to their third year of life, though high-ranking women and queens delegated this task to wet nurses who became an integral part of the family. The mother deity Isis herself was repeatedly depicted breastfeeding her son Horus.[23] The Ebers Papyrus describes the use of milk stimulant recipes including smearing the back with a mixture of ground Nile-perch bones fried in oil. Alternatively, the nursing mother ate bread made from soured durra with poppy plant.[24] The breastfeeding mother of course had further recourse to the deity Taueret.[25]

The basis of the economy and thus survival in the nomadic and agricultural tribes living in the Eastern Mediterranean was highly dependent on the size of the extended family or community. Numbers ensured that the community could produce sufficient resources for its survival and ensured its safety from attack from other neighbouring communities. Children were needed to ensure the parents" care in later life and ensure the performance of required burial rites to enable the enjoyment of everlasting life in the afterlife. It is no wonder that fertility was a highly prized "gift from the deities" who needed to be appeased and obeyed to retain their continuing benevolence.

---

[23] Schulz R, Seidel M., 2004, *op. cit.*
[24] Joachim H., 1860, *op. cit.*
[25] Sykes E., 1993, *op. cit.*

Punic & Egyptian Remains from Malta

The Phoenicians or Canaanites were an ancient Semitic people who from the fourth or beginning of the third millennium BC inhabited the eastern shores of the Mediterranean to the north of Mount Carmel, between Palestine and Syria. Throughout the history of the Phoenicians (including the western colony of Carthage), there is further to stereotyped inscriptions no literary evidence of Phoenician origin still extant, and hence our knowledge is derived from either archaeology or the writings of those who were their conquerors or their enemies. The Egyptian records are particularly informative, especially from the time of the IVth dynasty [2350-2180 BC] onwards. Phoenicia was engulfed by Egypt about 1525 BC. But towards the end of the second millennium BC, the irreversible decline of the pharaohs set in and the bonds keeping Phoenicia subject to Egypt loosened or fell away completely.

Unlike most ancient people, the Phoenicians were not primarily farmers, but already from the beginning of their known history sometime after 2900 BC, city dwellers and sailors. Possibly, the Phoenicians first launched their rafts and boats into the Mediterranean in search of food for an expanding population. Their land though fertile was tiny, but the sea was rich in food. Phoenician ships carried their trade westwards to the Mediterranean coasts and islands, sometimes substituting slave-raiding or piracy for trading, according to which yielded the best profit [26].

---

[26] S. Moscati: *The World of the Phoenicians*. London: Phoenix (Orion Books Ltd), 1999; H. Bondi, A. Bullock, W. Gordon, D. Piper, B. Williams (eds): *The Mind Alive Encyclopedia. Early Civilization*. London: Marshall Cavendish Books Ltd., 1977, p.33-36

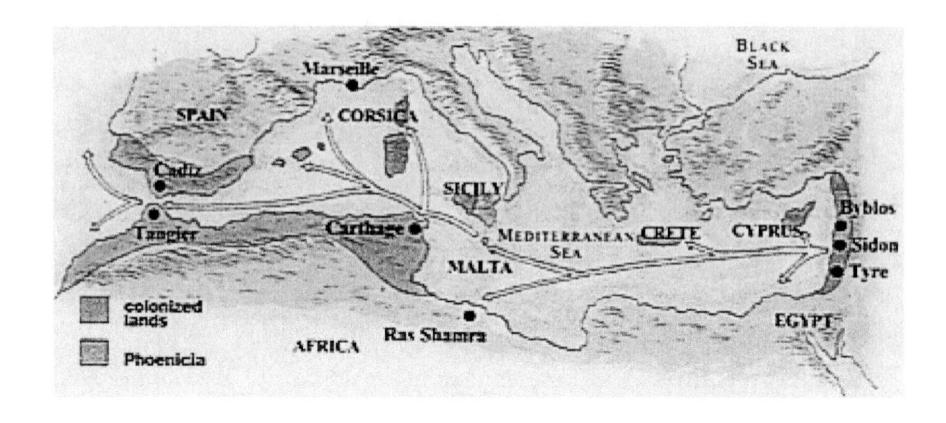

The earliest archaeological documentation for the Phoenician colonization of Malta dates to the late 8th to early 7th century BC. The Phoenician seafarers initially limited themselves to the utilization of the Islands as a port of call, but later gradually colonized the Islands. The most important of the north African colonies was Carthage, founded according to tradition in 814 BC as a result of a civil war that forced the population of Phoenicia to flee from Tyre. While the ties of the Phoenician colonies in the western Mediterranean with the mother country grew increasingly weaker, Carthage dominated the western Mediterranean until the city was finally destroyed by the Romans in 146 BC [27].

Thus, the Phoenician influence on the Islands was continued under the Carthaginians (circa 550 BC) who followed the steady decline of Phoenicia under the Assyrian and Neo-Babylonian empires circa 574 BC. The archaeological record of this phase remains Punic in type, though a number of Hellenistic importations

---

[27] S. Moscati, 1999: *op. cit.*; H. Bondi et al (eds), 1977: *op. cit.*

from Sicily and Southern Italy are increasingly noticeable. There is in addition archaeological evidence of an indirect Egyptian cultural connection [28].

We know little about the distinguishing characteristics of the Punic civilization in general, few traces of which remain. The Greeks credited the Phoenicians with the invention of the alphabet system of writing, and it seems likely that in the north-west Semitic languages, of which Phoenician and Hebrew were variants, lay the origin of the alphabets adapted by all Indo-European and Semitic languages. Phoenician literature certainly existed but has all disappeared like the language itself which seems to have persisted in some form up to the 3rd century AD. The Phoenician script was deciphered by Abbe' Bartehelemy on the basis of inscriptions cut into two marble cippi found in Malta and preserved in the National Archaeological Museum of Malta and in the Louvre in Paris, the latter having been donated to Louis XIV by Grandmaster De Rohan [*Corpus Inscriptionum Semiticarum I 122 and 122 bis*] [29].

Cippus CIS I 122; 122 bis

---

[28] T.C. Gouder: Phoenician Malta. *Heritage. An Encyclopædia of Maltese Culture and Civilization*, 1978, 1:173-186; T.C. Gouder: Some amulets from Phoenician Malta. *Heritage. An Encyclopædia of Maltese Culture and Civilization*, 1978, 1:311-315.

[29] T. Zammit: *Malta. The Maltese Islands and their history*. Malta: A.C. Aquilina Publ., 1971, 3rd ed. reprint, p. 62-66

Very little is known about the medical practices of the Phoenicians and Carthaginians, but it is recorded that one of the books of the Egyptian medical papyrus, the Ebers - written between 1550-1547 BC - was the work of an oculist from Byblos in Phoenicia. What we know of the book permits us to conjecture much more important knowledge than has been heretofore suspected in this Semitic race. They, and likewise the Carthaginians, believed that the daily hazards of existence were caused by a multitude of malevolent spirits who permeated the universe and intervened in natural processes. These spirits were thus responsible for the onset of disease. They were imagined as hideous grimacing beings that could be exorcised by the magical powers of amulets or by incantations written on small strips of papyrus. Ill health was very closely related to religion [30].

Punic Mythology: The Phoenicians had an array of supreme deities in their pantheon. There is definite evidence that the Maltese Punic population venerated some of these deities. Ba`al Hammon was the chief deity of Carthage, where he was depicted as a dignified old man with a beard, his head embellished with ram's horns. He was the sky-god and god of fertility[31]. His cult spread into the islands of Malta, Sicily and Sardinia. An inscribed cippus [*CIS I 123*], measuring 20.3 x 7.6 x 7.6cm found near St. Dominic's Convent in Rabat (Malta) dated to the 6th century BC, reads: "*stele of molk* (a technical term of sacrificial holocaust of a child) *to Ba`al set up by Nahum to the Lord Ba`al Hammon*". The twin cippi [*CIS I 122 and*

---

[30] J.H. Bass: *Outlines of the History of Medicine and the medical profession*. Huntington: R.E. Krieger Publ., 1971, p.29-30
[31] L. Delporte: Phoenician Mythology. *New Larousse Encyclopedia of Mythology*. London: Hamlyn Publ, 1981, p.73-84; J.H. Bass, 1971: *op. cit.*; E. Sykes: *Who's Who Non-Classical Mythology*. New York: Oxford University Press, 1993, p.25

122 bis], which enabled the decipherment of the Phoenician alphabet, were a dedication to Ba'al Melkart, the chief deity of Tyre transported to Carthage. The inscription reads "*A vow from Abdosir, and his brother Osirshamar, sons of Osirshamar, son of Abdosir, to my Lord Melkart, Lord of Tyre, that he may hear their words and bless them*"[32]. Claudius Ptolemeaus (Ptolemy), a 2nd century AD writer, mentions a temple in the southern region of Malta dedicated to Melkart (Hercules). Thought to have been situated at the Tas-Silg or Borg in-Nadur area, archaeological excavations have shown that these sites had different functions, and the location of the temple of Melkart remains unknown, though it has recently been suggested to have been located at Ras ir-Raheb [33].

Symbolic representation of Astarte from Dougga, Tunisia & Astarte's name inscribed on pottery shard form Tas-Silg, Malta

---

[32] H. Lewis: *Ancient Malta - A study of its antiquities*. Colin Smythe Ltd, Bucks, 1977, p.79-81; T.C. Gouder: 1978: *op. cit*

[33] A. Bonanno: Quintinus and the location of the Temple of Hercules at Marsaxlokk. *Melita Historica*, 1982, 8(3):190-204; N.C. Vella: The lie of the land: Ptolemy's temple of Heracles in Malta. *Ancient Near Eastern Studies*, 2002, 38 (forthcoming)

Ptolemy also refers to a sanctuary dedicated to the female Roman divinity Juno. The locality of this sanctuary has now been established at Tas-Silg in Marsaxlokk (Malta) where excavations carried out by an Italian Archaeological Mission from the University of Rome in the 1960s revealed several scores of inscriptions invoking the goddess Astarte, known also as Ashtar, Ishtar (to the Babylonians), Ashtoreth (to the Hebrews), and Tanit (to the Carthaginians). The Punic deity Astarte was equated with the Grecian deity Aphrodite and the Roman deity Venus. Astarte was the goddess of fertility of the Semites. Her domain embraced all nature, vegetable and animal as well as human. Afterwards she became the goddess of love in its noblest aspect as well as in its most degraded [34].

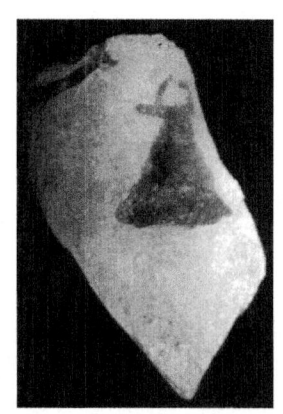

Pottery shard depicting Tanit, Tas-Silg, Malta

Head of Juno, Tas-Silg, Malta

---

[34] T.C. Gouder, 1978: *op. cit.*; A. Bonanno, 1982: *op. cit.*; J. Quintin d'Autun: *Insulae Melitae Descriptio*, Lyons, 1536 (facsimile ed. Malta: Bibliotheca), p.3-4; H.C.R. Vella: *The earliest description of Malta (Lyons 1536). Translation and Notes*. Malta: DeBono Enterprises, 1980, p.20-23; G.F. Abela: *Della descrittione di Malta isola nel Mare Siciliano con le sue antichita`*. Malta; Paolo Bonacota, 1647 (facsimile ed. Malta: Midsea Books, 1984), p.154-157; O. Bres: *Malta Antica Illustrata co' Monumenti e coll'Istoria*. Rome: Stamperia De Romanis, 1816 (facsimile ed. Malta: Midsea Books, 1986), p.70-147

The inscription *CIS I 123* makes specific mention a "*molk*" sacrificed to Ba`al Hammon. The term is generally taken to refer to child sacrifice generally performed at specialised sacrificial centres known as "tophets". Child sacrifice was a well-established practice of the Carthaginians performed in order to appease the Punic gods Ba`al Hammon and Tanit. "Tophets" have been unearthed through excavation not only in all the major Phoenician colonial sites of the Western Mediterranean but also in many sites surrounding the Maltese archipelago, including Sicily, Sardinia and Tunisia. A typical "tophet" may have been excavated at Rabat, Malta [35]. It is therefore highly probable that as the Phoenicians extended their trade routes westward reaching the Maltese Islands, they brought along with them the practice of child sacrifice from the East and introduced this in Malta and other western settlements. It would seem that the Phoenician population in the Maltese Islands did indulge in child sacrifice in times of crisis such as the Roman invasion of 218 BC. In a similar situation, Diodorus Siculus, a Sicilian-Greek historian writing about 45 BC, gave an account of the sacrifice of 500 children in 310 BC when the city of Carthage was under attack by the Sicilian Greeks. Excavations at the shrine of Tanit at Salammbo (near Carthage) have revealed cinerary urns containing the cremated remains of young children [36].

The Punic culture in Malta showed evidence of cultural links to Egyptian mythology. Thus, Egyptian fertility-related deities are known to have been venerated by the Punic Maltese. Talismans in the form of faience amulet figurines representing Bes and Toueris

---

[35] M. Shortland-Jones: The Phoenician Connection. *Treasures in Malta*, 1998 5(1):p.92.
[36] S. Moscati, 1999: *op. cit.*; H. Bondi et al (eds), 1977: *op. cit.*, p.36

have been excavated from tombs in Malta and Gozo. Bes, an African deity by origin, was a popular god known also in Egypt and western Asia. He was a frightening dwarf with bow-legs, a prominent belly, and an animal-like face with bulging eyes. He was frequently clothed with a panther skin with claws, sported a distinctive headdress, and wore a metal disc around his neck. This made him a veritable collection of apotropaic implements, and he was better equipped than anybody else to frighten away and chase off evil spirits and neutralize the evil eye. People therefore had him around whenever they felt particularly exposed to the spirits, and the parturient woman was considered to be at particular risk of falling prey to evil spirits because of her weakness and preoccupation. Bes thus presided over childbearing and was considered as a protector of expectant mothers. He was also a marriage-god and presided over the toilet of women [37].

Toueris was another popular protective Egyptian goddess of childbirth, and symbolized maternity and suckling. She herself had given birth to the world. Toueris was represented as a female hippopotamus with pendant mammae standing upright on her back legs and holding the hieroglyphic sign of protection in one paw and the sign of life in the other [38].

---

[37] J. Viaud: Egyptian Mythology. *New Larousse Encyclopedia of Mythology*. Hamlyn Publ, London, 1981, p.9-48; H.E. Sigerist: *A History of Medicine. Vol. I: Primitive and Archiac Medicine*. Oxford University Press, New York, 1951, p.241-242; C. Savona-Ventura: *Outlines of Maltese Medical History*. Malta, Midsea Publ., 1997, p.8-9; C. Savona-Ventura: Punic Mythology and Medicine. *Treasures of Malta*, 2002, 8(3):p.83-88

[38] J. Viaud, 1981: *op. cit.;* H.E. Sigerist, 1951: *op. cit.*; C. Savona-Ventura, 1997: *op. cit.*; C. Savona-Ventura, 2002: *op. cit*

Bes - Xewkija, Gozo 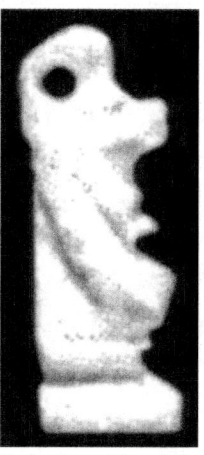   *Toieris – Xewkija, Gozo*    *Ptah-Patecus*

Besides the faience amulets depicting Bes and Toueris found at Tal-Horob, Xewkija (Gozo), other amulets depicting the Ugiat, Ptah-Patecus and Amon-Ra - king of the gods, creator of the universe - were excavated. The deity Ptah-Patecus is here depicted in his alternative form as a deformed dwarf with twisted legs, hands on hips and a huge head shaved except for the childish lock. Thus represented, Ptah-Patecus plays the role of protector against noxious animals and against all kinds of evil [39].

The Punic Underworld: The Punic Maltese were concerned not only with birth and fertility, but also with death. In Phoenician mythology, Death was conceived as a supernatural power called Muth. This was however never worshipped because it played no part in any Phoenician religious cult. The Phoenicians believed in an

---

[39] T.C. Gouder, 1978a: *op. cit.*, p.312; J. Viaud, 1981, *op. cit.*, p.36; C. Savona-Ventura, 2002: *op. cit.*

afterlife and in the long sea-voyage that led the deceased to the world of the dead [40]. These beliefs are evidenced by the care given to their tombs containing grave-goods and the Egyptian-style talismans associated with death. A sixth-century BC bronze amulet sheath containing a small rolled-up piece of papyrus bearing a Phoenician inscription with a representation to Isis was found in a tomb at Tal-Virtu`, limits of Rabat (Malta). The sheath with a cover in the form of a falcon's head representing Horus - the Egyptian solar divinity - belongs to a distinct class manufactured in rigid imitation of Egyptian prototypes and widely diffused in Phoenicia and its colonies. The inscription has been translated to read "*laugh at your enemy O valiant ones, scorn, assail and crush your adversary ...disdain (him), trample (him) on the waters; ...moreover prostate (him) ...on the sea, bind (him), hang (him)*". These are the words of Isis - the sorrowing wife and eternal mother, protectress of the dead - addressed to the deceased and which ensured her assistance for an unfailing victory over a mythical adversary barring the way to the afterlife. Isis is in the papyrus represented bearing a throne upon her head, the ideogram of her name. In the various Egyptian medical texts, Isis is shown to have held an important place in the pantheon of healing dieties. Her legend is full of episodes of magic cures, and repeatedly she appears as the great magician whose counsel is the breath of life, whose sayings drive out sickness, and whose word gives life to him whose breath is failing. Isis was adopted by the Romans when she was considered a healing goddess, discoverer of drugs, versed in the art of curing people who flocked to her temples,

---

[40] A.J. Frendo, A. de Trafford, N.C. Vella: Water Journeys of the Dead: a glimpse into Phoenician and Punic eschatology. In Atti del V Congresso Internazionale di Studi Fenici e Punici, Palermo-Marsala, 2-8 ottobre 2000.

lying down in the halls, expecting to be delivered of their ailments by the goddess in their sleep [41].

Amulet depicting Horus and papyrus with prayer to Isis

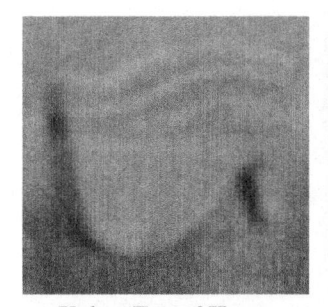

Ugiat: Eye of Horus　　*Thoth*

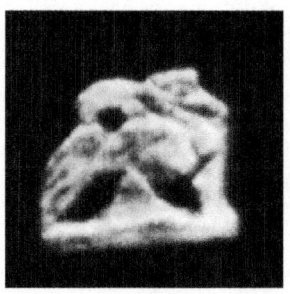

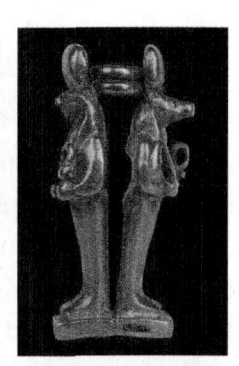

Horus & Anubis

---

[41] T.C. Gouder, B. Rocco: Un talismano bronzeo da Malta contenente un nastro di papiro con iscrizione fenicia. *Studi Magrebini*, VII, 1975, p.1-18; T.C. Gouder, 1978a: *op. cit.*; J. Viaud, 1981: *op. cit.*; E. Sykes, 1993: *op. cit.*, p.97-98; H.E. Sigerist, 1951: *op. cit.*, p.288

Horus, son of Isis and Osiris, was the falcon-headed sky god. The mythical story of his fight with Seth, established Horus as the god of the sun and god of life and of all good. During his battle against Seth, Horus has his eye gouged out. This was later restored by the deity Thoth. The eye of Horus (the Ugiat) remained a magical talisman for health throughout Egyptian history. The British Museum Medical Papyrus written at the end of the XVIIIth Dynasty (circa 14th century BC) records how the Ugiat was invoked while applying a remedy to diseased eyes with the following charm recited four times. *"This Eye of Horus created by the spirits of Heliopolis, which Thoth has brought from Hermopolis – from the great hall in Heliopolis, - in Pe,- in Dep, sayest thou to it: 'Welcome, thou splendid Eye of Horus, - thou content of the Eye of Horus – brought to drive out evil of the god, the evil of goddess, the demon, male and female, the dead, male and female, the enemy, male and female, who have insinuated themselves into the eyes of the sick under my fingers. – Protection, behind me protection, come protection!"*

Horus had also been stung by a deadly scorpion and was saved by the powerful spells of the gods. He thus was considered to have himself acquired special facilities to cure people bitten by venomous animals. There have also been several amulets depicting the Ugiat excavated from various sites in Malta and Gozo (eg. the faience amulets excavated from Tal-Horob, Xewkija (Gozo) in 1951 dated c.5th-4th century BC. A gold amulet excavated from Ghajn Klieb, west of Rabat (Malta) depicts the figure of falcon-headed Horus and jackal-headed Anubis. The two figures were in antiquity soldered together at the base and the top. In spite of their strikingly Egyptian appearance, the figures are considered to be very probably of eastern Phoenician manufacture. Anubis was the Egyptian deity who presided over the embalming of the dead. The name signifies watcher and guardian of the dogs. He presided over the abode of the dead, led the deceased to the judgement hall and supervised the weighing of the heart. Amulets depicting ibis-headed or dog-headed ape Thoth have also been found in Maltese tombs. In the introduction to the Ebers Papyrus, it is stated that "*I* (Re, the sun god) *will save him from his enemies, and Thoth shall be his guide, he who lets writing speak and has composed books; he gives to the skilful, to the physicians who accompany him, skill to cure.*" Thoth was considered a great physician and magician acting as physician to the god Horus. He was regarded as the god of magic, and was the arbiter between the gods and had the knowledge needed by the dead to pass safely through the underworld [42].

Related to the cult of the afterlife were faience amulets depicting the Djed and Ouaz pillars dated to the 7th-6th century BC excavated from Bingemma near Rabat (Malta). The Djed pillar, symbol of stability, seemingly originated from the form of a column of bound papyrus, was a simple fetish representing Osiris - god of the dead. Osiris gave his devotees the hope of an eternally happy life in another world ruled over by a just and good king. The Ouaz pillar derived from the form of the lotus flower was the symbol of rebirth [43].

---

[42] T.C. Gouder, 1978a: *op. cit.*; T. Gouder: Fuq xi Amuleti minn Malta Fenicjo-Punika. In: T. Cortis (ed.) *Oqsma tal-Kultura Malitja. Kungress Nazzjonali 18-19 ta' April 1991.* Malta: Ministry of Education, 1991, p.67-82; J. Viaud, 1981: *op. cit.*; E. Sykes, 1993: *op. cit.*, p.13,69,88-89; B. Brier: *Egyptian Mummies. Unraveling the Secrets of an Ancient Art.* M. London: O'Mara Books Ltd., 1996, p.27; H.E. Sigerist, 1951, *op. cit.*, p.285-288

[43] T.C. Gouder, 1978a: *op. cit.*; J. Viaud, 1981: *op. cit.*

Djed & Ouaz pillars representing Osiris

Punic Burial Practices: While little is known about the actual medical practice of the Punic Maltese further than their preoccupation with malevolent spirits, the community was well aware of the public health necessity of prohibiting burials within the city walls. Carthaginian customs and eventually Roman laws were strongly adverse to intramural burials, hence the rule "*hominem mortuum in urbe ne sepelito neve urito*" meaning "human bodies should neither be buried nor burnt within the town"[44]. These extra-mural burials gave rise in Malta to a number of necropolises in the periphery of the ancient capital of Melite with about 343 tombs, and the Paola-Marsa maritime habitations. In Gozo the greatest cluster of tombs were found around Victoria. Until the mid-1990s,

---

[44] T. Zammit: *The St. Paul's Catacombs and other rock-cut tombs in Malta.* 7th ed. Union Press, Malta, 1980, p.10

archaeological excavations had brought to light a total of 649 Punic tombs in Malta, 18 tombs in Gozo and one in Comino. The tombs structure was of four basic types: (1) the shaft and chamber tombs; (2) the shaft tomb; (3) the chamber tomb; and (4) the grave pit. The first type was the most common tomb whereby the rectangular or oval burial chamber was preceded by an open generally rectangular shaft measuring in average 1.7m in length, 0.8m in width and 1.5m in height. Only about 35 shaft rectangular or circular tombs have been described in the Maltese Islands. After internment, these tombs were roofed by some closing slabs. The chamber tomb, best exemplified by the tombs at Bingemma (Malta) dated to circa 1st century BC, were usually hewn in the vertical face of the rock. This oval tomb had an average height of about 0.9m. The grave pit tombs were either rock-cut or soil depressions. These were usually intended for cremation burials [45].

The increasing preoccupation with the afterlife had resulted in a change in burial practices. During the Phoenician-Punic Period, in the Maltese Islands the dead were either inhumed or cremated, as was customary in all the other parts of the Phoenician-Punic world. In the earlier phase of the Phoenician occupation, cremation seems to have been the commoner practice. During the Carthaginian period (c.550-300 BC) burial by inhumation predominated, though evidence of sporadic cremation still occurs. In the late Punic Phase, while inhumation remained the most common form of burial, cremation became increasingly more popular. Many of the tombs were re-utilized during the centuries and sometimes had both

---

[45] T. Zammit, 1980: *op. cit.*, p.3-11; G.A. Said-Zammit: Maltese Antiquities. Punic Tombs of Malta and Gozo. . *Heritage. An Encyclopedia of Maltese Culture and Civilization*, 1999, 5:1529-1534; G.A. Said-Zammit: *Population land use and settlement on Punic Maltas: a contextual analysis of the burial evidence*. Oxford: BAR, 1997.

cremated remains and inhumations. One of the earliest Punic tombs excavated at Ghajn Qajjet (Rabat, Malta) contained two inhumation burials dated to the late 8th to early 7th century BC. During the early 1st century BC a cinerary urn with cremated remains was apparently deposited in the same tomb. The latest Punic tombs have been dated to circa early 1st century AD when the Islands were already under Roman rule. Tomb furniture varied according to the period. It was simple in the early days but later on it became more abundant with numerous clay vases, glass bottles, ivory and metal objects being deposited with the dead for use in the afterlife [46]. While cremated remains were generally deposited in cinerary urns, inhumation burials were generally laid out in the tombs, usually in an extended position on the back without being placed in a coffin or wrapped in a shroud. Since the late 4th century BC, the calcined human remains started to be deposited in a standard type of locally manufactured cinerary urns. The average height of these urns was about 35cm, whilst the average diameter was approximately 28cm. These urns have normally a sinuous body, a flat rim, a convex lip, and sometimes the lower part of the body leads to an extended flat or concave base. They also normally have two vertical ear-shaped handles on the upper part of the body, though some urns are single-handled. The form of this particular urn survived until the 1st century AD, though with some stylistic modifications.

---

[46] G.A. Said-Zammit, 1999: *op. cit.*; T. Zammit, 1980: *op. cit.*, p.3-11

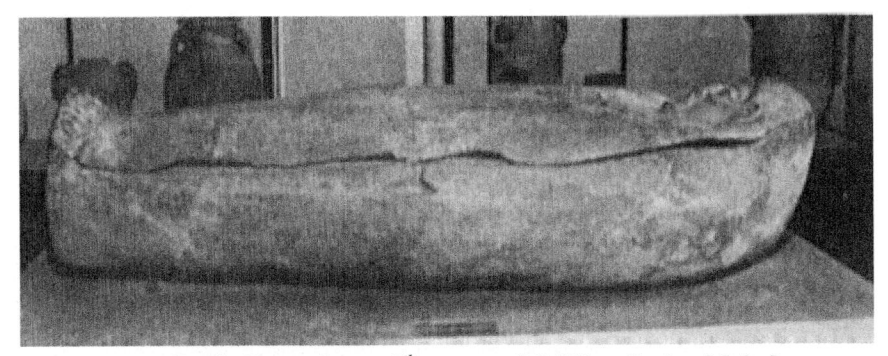

Punic Sarcophagus 5th century BC [Ghar Barka, Malta]

Occasionally the body was placed in purpose-designed sarcophagi or in a large amphora. From Malta and Gozo there is evidence of five terracotta sarcophagi, of which only two survive and conserved in the National Museum of Archaeology at Valletta. The tomb at Ghar Barka (Rabat, Malta) discovered in 1797 yielded three of the sarcophagi. The tomb consisted of a square shaft and a square chamber. One sarcophagus is a long terracotta anthropomorphic container measuring 1.56 metres in length. It has been dated to the early 5th century BC. The style of the sarcophagus is Egyptian, though the head has a markedly Rhodian-Ionian imprint. The non-anthropoid sarcophagus is rectangular in form with a cover consisting of three terracotta slabs. It has been dated to the late 4th or early 3rd century BC. Two other sarcophagi, one of which was anthropoid, were found from undisclosed sites in Gozo. A supposed Punic burial discovered in Comino in 1912 utilized a split amphora to cover the skeleton. One portion of the amphora covered the body from head to waist, the other portion covered the rest though the feet and a small portion of the legs protruded. Embalming, another type of Phoenician burial reserved for kings and princes, is unknown in Malta [47].

Medical Disorders: Medical disorders prevalent on the Islands during the Punic Period can be identified from the skeletal material excavated from the various tombs. Unfortunately, little definite dating has accompanied archaeological excavation of Classical Age skeletal material and therefore it is difficult to identify the age of any pathological material and assign this to the Punic period.

Six Punic or Phoenician skulls studied by R.N. Bradley in 1912 were described as being ellipsoid (1), beloid (2), ovoid (1), and pentagoid (2). One of the skulls pictured showed the presence of a partial metopic suture. The frontal bone is ossified in fibrous tissue from two primary centres that appear in the eight-week of intrauterine life. From each of these centres ossification extends upwards to form the corresponding half of the bone. At birth the bone consists of two halves separated by the frontal or metopic suture, but union begins in the second year, and the suture is usually completely obliterated by the eighth year. In a percentage of persons which shows some racial variation, the two halves of the frontal bone remain separate, and the metopic suture persists [48].

---

[47] T.C. Gouder, 1978: op. cit., p.177; T. Zammit: Grave at Comino Island. *Reports on the Workings of Government Department during the financial year 1911-12*. Malta: Government Printing Office, 1912, p.E4; G. A. Said-Zammit: The Punic Tombs of the Maltese Islands. *Proceedings of History Week 1993* (ed. K. Sciberras). Malta: Malta Historical Society, 1997, p.67-80.

[48] R.N. Bradley: *Malta and the Mediterranean Race*. London: T. Fisher Unwin, 1912, pg.175, fig.41-44; R. Warwick, P.L. Williams PL (eds.): *Gray's Anatomy*, Edinburgh: Longman, 35th edition, 1973, p.299-300

The Ghajn Tuffieha skulls excavated by J.S. Swann circa 1865 and described by J. Thurnam showed some possibly pathological features[49]. This series of four tombs yielded the remains of at least eight interred individuals, presumably three males, three females and two children. Cremated remains were also found contained in pottery jars.

The skulls from Tomb 1 suggested elderly individuals, the male aged circa 70-75 years while the female aged circa 65 years. The first skull was described as having a considerable degree of prognathism while the chin was narrow and rather prominent. The most remarkable feature of this skull was the great prominence of the nasals that were directed outwards and forwards at an almost right angle at the glabella. The estimated Cephalic Index and the Height-Length Indices are given as 74 and 77 respectively. Only two teeth remained in the upper jaw, the majority being lost antemortem. The lower jaw had only the left canine remaining, this being the seat of much jagged erosion. The second skull obtained from the same tomb had more feminine characteristics and similarly showed a certain degree of proganthism. The teeth remaining in the lower jaw showed a considerable degree of attrition. The estimated Cephalic Index and the Height-Length Indices are given as 78 and 78 respectively. The long bones of the excavated skeletons were measured (Table 1) and the height of the individuals estimated at circa 61 inches (154.94cm).

---

[49] J.S. Swann: Description of Ancient Rock-Tombs at Ghajn Tiffiha and Tal Horr, Malta. *Archeologia*, 1870, XL: p.483-487; J. Thurnam: On the human remains and especially the Skull from the Rock-Tombs at Ghain Tiffiha and Tal Horr, and from other places in Malta. *Archeologia*, 1870, XL: p.488-499

Long bone Measurement (mm.)	Tomb 1 A	Tomb 1 B	Tomb 2	Tomb 3 A	Tomb 3 B
Femur	413	413	-	-	-
Tibia	355	349	-	381	374
Fibula	-	343	-	-	-
Humerus	308	-	317	-	-
Radius	241	216	237	247	241
Ulna	260	235	-	-	-

Table 1: Measurements – Ghajn Tuffieha long-bones

Excavated also in 1865 by J.S. Swann, the Tal-Horr rock-tomb was a relatively deep-shafted tomb that yielded the remains and skulls of three individuals. One of the skulls was studied and described by J. Thurnam. This skull belonged to a male individual aged 50 years or younger. The skull showed a slight tendency towards prognathism shown in the eversion of the short dental arcade of the intermaxillaries. The lower jaw showed a prominent and somewhat pointed chin. An unusual number of teeth, especially those of the lower jaw, appear to have been lost antemortem. Based on cranial measurements in inches, Thurnam estimated the Cephalic Index and the Height-Length Indices as 75 and 78 respectively [50]. Re-measurement of the Tal-Horr skull, now kept in the University of Cambridge (UK), estimated the indices as 77.54 and 76.47 respectively. Other skulls described and measured by J. Thurnam included (1) a specimen obtained by M. Fresnel in 1847 from the Bingemma rock-cut tombs and described by D. Wilson in 1862-63; and (2) a specimen obtained from a rock-cut catacomb in Malta and kept in the Lund Museum (Table 2) [51].

---

[50] J.S. Swann, 1870: *op. cit.*; J. Thurnam, 1870: *op. cit.*
[51] J.S. Swann, 1870: *op. cit.*; J. Thurnam, 1870: *op. cit.* Thurnam included the Hagar Qim skull generally considered as Neolithic. This skull was found imbedded in the detritus

MEASUREMENT (inches)	Ghajn Tuffieha A	Ghajn Tuffieha B	Bingemma	Tal-Horr	Undefined (Lund Museum)
Sex	M	F?	F	M	M
Age (est.)	75	65	-	50	-
Cranial Length	7.4	6.9	7.4	7.5	-
Cranial Breadth	5.5p	5.4t	5.1	5.65p	-
Cranial Height	5.7	5.4	5.3	5.9	-
Circumference	20.8	20	20.2	21.3	-
Facial Length	4.2	4.1	-	4.1	-
Facial Breadth	5.3	5.3	-	5.2	-
Cranial Index	74	78	69	75	80
Vertical Index	77	78	71	78	-
Capacity	98	75	-	100	-

Table 2: Measurement of Classical Skulls by J. Thurnam

Epidemic disease has also been described as affecting warring troops in neighbouring Sicily during the siege of Syracuse in 396 BC and during the Second Punic war of 212 BC. These epidemics, particularly the latter, could easily have extended to the Maltese community.

---

at a depth of two feet above the floor within the Neolithic Temple of Hagar Qim together with a quantity of quadruped and few human bones during excavations in conducted 1839. The characteristic feature of this skull was its marked prognathism and its rather negroid characteristics. Thurnam measurements gave a recalculated CI value of 78.6, a Height-Length Index of 77.1, and a Height-Breadth Index of 98.2. The skull was subsequently measured by T. Zammit who reported a CI of 77.7, and a Height-Length Index of 72.7 – vide T. Zammit, T.E. Peet and R.N. Bradley: *The small objects and the human skulls found in the Hal Saflieni prehistoric Hypogeum at Casal Paula, Malta.* Malta, 1912, p.29

Date	Disease	Locality
396 BC	? Smallpox/Plague	**Sicily**: Disease afflicted the Carthaginian army as it besieged Syracuse.
212 BC	? Influenza	**Sicily**: Outbreak of disease among Roman troops and Carthaginian defenders during the siege of Syracuse during the Second Punic War.

INFECTIOUS EPIDEMICS IN MEDITERRANEAN BASIN

Old Kingdom artefacts: The Egyptianizing movement mentioned above postdates the Egyptian Old Kingdom and date to the Maltese Punic or Semitic Period which commenced with the initial contacts made by the inhabitants of the islands with the Phoenician traders from the east around 700 BCE. The Phoenicians were an ancient Semitic people who from the fourth or beginning of the third millennium BCE inhabited the eastern shores of the Mediterranean to the north of Mount Carmel, between Palestine and Syria. Unlike most ancient people, the Phoenicians were not primarily farmers, but already from the beginning of their known history sometime after 2900 BCE, city dwellers and sailors. Possibly, the Phoenicians first launched their rafts and boats into the Mediterranean in search of food for an expanding population. Their land though fertile was tiny, but the sea was rich in food. Phoenician ships carried their trade westwards to the Mediterranean coasts and islands, sometimes substituting slave-raiding or piracy for trading, according to which yielded the best profit.[52]

The Phoenicians assimilated the artistic and iconographic heritage of the Egyptian culture, often changing radically its original meaning. The earliest archaeological documentation for the Phoenician colonization of Malta dates to the late 8th to early 7th century BCE. The Phoenician seafarers initially limited themselves to the utilization of the Islands as a port of call, but later gradually colonized the Islands. The contact with this Semitic culture allowed for the introduction of the Punic culture to the Maltese population. The Egyptianizing movement during the Punic Age in Malta is evidenced by the large number of amulets depicting Egyptian deities.[53]

This cultural phase persisted and became more prevalent during the Carthaginian Period which lasted from about 550 BCE to 218 BCE when the islands fell under Roman dominion after the Second Punic War when Tiberius Sempronius Longus crossed from Sicily in search of the Carthaginian fleet to secure his southern flank. The Roman invasion initially had very little cultural influence on the Islands, and for a couple of centuries the Punic substratum can be detected in the archaeological record.

These cultural concepts were to persist long after the advent of the Romans on the Islands during the Second Punic War in 218 BCE. A second Egyptianizing movement occurred during the Roman

---

[52] S. Moscati: The World of the Phoenicians. London: Phoenix (Orion Books Ltd), 1999
[53] C. Savona-Ventura: Punic Mythology and Medicine. Treasures of Malta, 2002, 8(3): p.83-88

Period. It has been standard practice to assume all Egyptianized archaeological remains to belong to the Punic or Roman period [54]; however, some individual items need to be re-examined since their stylistic elements place these to the second millennium BCE, centuries before the accepted Punic contact of the Maltese community.

The second millennium BCE in Malta was characterized by a Bronze Age community. Following the collapse of the Late Neolithic Temple Culture in the Maltese Islands about 2500 BCE, the islands were apparently left unpopulated for several centuries. They were subsequently progressively colonized in successive waves by a new cultural population who brought with them a metallurgical technology. The first phase of the Bronze Age is represented by the cremation cemetery at Tarxien. The Tarxien Cemetery [TC] culture introduced metallurgy, cremation burial and new pottery. Radiocarbon dating of carbonized horse-beans from TC deposits has given a dating of 1930 ± 150 BCE. The culture was to linger well into the second millennium BCE, slowly building up its population. The origins of these settlers have not been fully determined, but their pottery and clay idols show highly stylized forms with affinities to Mycenean idols and Anatolian and Cycladic types, affinities that suggest cultural links with communities from

---

[54] A. Bonanno: An Egyptianizing Relief from Malta. Egitto in Italia, dall'Antichita` al Medioevo`. Atti del III Congresso Internazionale Italo-Egiziano, Roma, CNR - Pompei, 13-19 Novembre 1995 [eds. N. Bonacasa, M.C. Naro, E.C. Portale, A. Tullio]. Consiglio Nazionale delle Ricerche, Roma, 1998, p.217-228; A. Bonanno: The Archaeology of Gozo: from Prehistoric to Arab Times. In: Gozo: The Roots of an Island. (ed. C. Cini), Said International, Malta, 1990, p. 11-46; A. Bonanno: Roman Malta. The Archaeological heritage of the Maltese Islands. World Conf. Salesian Past Pupils, Lugano, 1992, p.13-17.

the Aegean possibly via Sicily.[55] Thus pottery forms from the Tarxien Cemetery site excavations show links to the Early Bronze Age Capo Graziano ware from Lipari and the Early Helladic Western Greece and Dalmatia. Other TC pottery ware bears very close parallels with Thermi on the island of Lesbos, off the Dardanelles in the northern Aegean with others from the Second City of Troy. CT pottery ware may have been exported to Sicily and Syracuse.[56]

The second Maltese Bronze Age phase (circa 1500-700 BCE) takes its name from a Bronze Age village at Borg in-Nadur, which was fortified by a massive wall of "cyclopean" style on one side. The characteristic sites of the Borg in-Nadur culture are the promontory and hill-top settlements. It seems possible that this wave of immigrants came from Sicily, though Borg in-Nadur vessels showed affinities to Thapsos and Mycenaean ware.[57] An intrusive group during this latter phase was the Bahrija Phase (circa 900-700 BCE), whose pottery suggests an origin or a strong cultural attachment from the Iron Age of southern Italy, Apulia or Calbria.[58]

No definite Egyptian cultural links have been identified in the Maltese Bronze Age communities. However spectrographic studies carried out by Dr. J.F.S. Stone on a series of faience disc beads excavated by Sir. Temi Zammit from the Bronze Age [TC] deposits

---

[55] D.H. Trump: Malta: An Archaeological Guide. Progress Press, 1990, p.31; A. Bonanno, 1990: op. cit., p. 11-46
[56] D.H. Trump & D. Cilia: Malta. Prehistory and Temples. Midsea Books Ltd., Malta, 2002, p.248-249
[57] J.D. Evans: The Prehistoric Antiquities of the Maltese Islands. A survey. Athlone Press, London, 1971, p.226; D.H. Trump: The Prehistory of the Mediterranean. Pelican Books, Suffolk (UK), 1981, p.214-215
[58] J.D. Evans, 1971: op. cit., p.227

at Tarxien suggested that one small segmented almost transparent turquoise-blue bead had close characteristics to the Egyptian product of the 18th Dynasty [1580-1314 BCE].[59] This scientific association alone should promote further searches in the Maltese archaeological record to establish the possibility of other cultural links to Dynastic Egypt.

During this period, the Egyptian empire had dominated the entire known world including the Mediterranean "islands of the great circle" Crete, Cyprus and the Cyclades. A possible cultural link between the Maltese Islands and the Egyptian empire was originally proposed in 1806 by Federico Munter, Professor of Theology at the University of Copenhagen.[60] This link had both its proponents and opponents. Sir Temi Zammit in 1919 wrote that "*Traces of Egyptian art have been met with in the Island, and this led some writers to believe in an Egyptian occupation. This conclusion cannot be accepted, but that an extensive intercourse with the Egyptians existed, is admitted. During the reign of Tothmes III (BC1500-1450), the Egyptians sailed all along the Mediterranean and effected landings on nearly all the shores of this sea. The Phoenicians themselves were great carriers of Egyptian wares*".[61] In 1928 the renowned Egyptologist Margaret Murray again proposed that "*there are traces of the connexions* [sic] *in the XIIth dynasty with Malta and even further west*" predating the links with Crete. Murray

---

[59] J.F.S. Stone: Faience Beads from the Tarxien Cemetery. In: J.D. Evans, 1971: op. cit., p.235-236

[60] F. Munter: Aegyptischer religisbregriffe in Sicilien und den benachbarten inseln. Lecture presented to the Societa` Reale delle Scienze di Boemia, 1806. In: O. Bres: Malta Antica illustrata co' Monumenti e coll' Istoria. Stamperia de Romanis, Rome, 1816, p.284-285

[61] T. Zammit: Guide to the Valletta Museum with a historical summary. Government Printing Office, Malta, 1919, p.9-10

stylistically assigned a number of archaeological finds with Egyptian features from the Maltese Islands to the 2nd millennium BCE.[62]

Evidence for the possible presence of an Egyptian-style cultural community in Malta with inhumation burials during the 2nd millennium BCE Tarxien Cemetery phase is furnished by the four Egyptian-type burial stele with cartouches excavated during the building of Bighi Hospital in 1829. The discovery was mentioned by W.K. Bedford in 1894 who wrote that "*in digging the foundations of which, Captain [afterwards Sir Harry] Smith R.G. discovered the Egyptian inscriptions now in the British Museum*". Sir Temi Zammit, two decades later, repeats this assertion. These were "donated" to the British Museum in 1836 by the Clerk of Works Mr. J.B. Collins.[63] They are still housed in the Department of Ancient Egypt and Sudan of the British Museum [U.K.] catalogued with the inventory numbers EA218, EA233, EA287, and EA299.[64] They have been arbitrary assumed by G. Holbl as having been introduced in Malta in

---

[62] M.A. Murray: Egyptian objects found in Malta. Ancient Egypt. 13[1928]: p.45-48; M.A. Murray: The Splendour that was Egypt. The New English Library Ltd., London, 1962, p.257-258

[63] A label superimposed on a contemporary photograph taken in Malta by Richard Ellis reads "Facsimile of a stele in Malta sandstone found in December 1829 when sinking for the foundations of the Naval Hospital at Bighi Malta. The original is in the Egyptian Gallery of the British Museum, No. 235, given by Mr. J.B. Collins of H.M. Da... in 1836 through Capt, (afterwards) General Sir Jones R. E.". Reported in: C. Testa: Prehistoric Antiquities. Egyptian Stele at Bighi. Heritage, n.d., 74: p.1473-1477; W.K. Bedford: Malta and the Knights Hospitallers. Seeley & Co., London, 1894, p.75; T. Zammit, 1919: op. cit., p.43. T. Zammit erroneously dated the Bighi find to 1864. He subsequently corrected the date to 1830. T. Zammit: Malta. The Maltese Islands and their history. 1st ed. 1926; 3rd ed. 1952, A.C. Aquilina, Malta, p.285

[64] R.B. Parkinson: Egyptian remains from Malta. e-mail to C. Savona-Ventura dated 20th August 2003.

modern times [65], possibly having served as ballast on cargo ships.[66] A visual and microfossil comparative study of the rock making up the stelae with rock from the Bighi district carried out at the British Museum showed that the stone making up the stelae was distinctly different from the Maltese limestone.[67] This tends to suggest an importation of the items in modern times or in antiquity.

The hieroglyphics on the four stele were eventually deciphered by Margaret Murray in 1928, who showed that these represented burial memorials. The inscriptions, consisting of prayers to Osiris dedicated to the spirit of a number of male and female personages, suggest that the locality was a cemetery for an Egyptian colony that believed in an after-life. The inscriptions have been by common consensus dated to the 18th dynasty 1580-1314 BCE with the exception of stele EA233 which refers to the 12th dynasty 1991-1785 BCE king Amenemhat III.[68]

The three 18th dynasty stelae respectively dedicated to the female *Harem-hesit* [EA218], the man *Thuy* [EA299]; and of the scribe *Teta-ty* [EA287] are stylistically similar. The former two are near-identical showing the shen-sign between the two sacred eyes

---

[65] G. Holbl: Agyptisches Kulturgut auf den Inseln Malta und Gozo in Phonikischer und Punischer Zeit. Vienna, 1989, p.168; A. Bonanno, 1998: op. cit.
[66] R.B. Parkinson, 2003: op. cit. The British Museum also regards these artefacts as being made in Egypt and transported to Malta in the modern period, possibly as ballast on cargo ships.
[67] R.B. Parkinson, 2003: op. cit.; A. Middleton: correspondence to C. Savona-Ventura dated 7th November 2003 and 23rd March 2004; Young J, Marée M, Cartwright C, Middleton A. Egyptian stelae from Malta. British Museum Technical Report Bulletin 2009, 3: p.23-30.
[68] M.A. Murray, 1928: op. cit.; R.B. Parkinson, 2003: op. cit. Confirms the stylistic dating to the 18th Dynasty for stele 218, 287, 299; and 12th Dynasty for stele 233 which mentions king Amenemhat III.

followed by a depiction of the kneeling or seated named deceased holding the lotus flower, and the persons [*Nub-nefert* and *Yb-Ymentet* respectively] who had set up the dedication thus causing the name of the deceased to live; below is carved a prayer that when extrapolated probably read "*May Osiris, this Ruler of eternity, give a royal offering. May he give funeral offerings of bread and beer, oxen and birds, and all things good and pure, for the ka of ....*". The last stele of this group shows the figure of enthroned Osiris, below whom is a table of offerings and kneeling worshipper. The prayer in this case is similar to the previous except that instead of funeral offerings of bread, beer, oxen and birds; the offerings included "*sweet breezes to the north, cool water, wine, milk, alabasters, linen*".

The stele assigned to the 12th dynasty [EA233] is stylistically completely different from the previous ones. The upper part carries a vertical cartouche reading "*The good god, Ne-maat-Re*". This is followed on the right by a couchant jackal on perch holding an ankl and three vertical lines of hieroglyphics that read "*Beloved of Wep-wawet, lord of the necropolis*". Further on the left is the standing figure of Osiris holding the was-sceptre and ankh and two vertical lines of hieroglyphs that read "*Beloved of Khenti-Amentiu, lord of Adbydos*". Below are ten horizontal lines of inscriptions that relate a prayer for the ka of several personages that may have belonged to the same family. The inscription reads "*O ye who live upon earth, every wab-priest, every lector-priest, every scribe, every ka-servant who pass by this endowed stele for ever: ye who love your life and your king, ye who praise your city-gods, ye who transmit your offices to your children, say ye, May Osiris, lord of Abdyos, give royal offering (may he give the funeral offering of bread and beer, oxen and birds, alabasters and linen, incense and perfume), All things good and pure, which heaven gives, which the earth produces, which the Nile brings, and on which the god lives, For the ka of the coppersmith Ankef, born of Kenyuyt; for the ka of Yfert, born of Ameny; for the ka of Yupy, born of Yfert; for the ka of Meres-Tekh, born of Yf(ert); for the ka of Atet, born of Yfert; for the ka of N.....; for the ka of Senenu, born of .....; for the ka of R......".*

In his review, C. Testa emphasises that the specific mention of definite female personages [*Harem-hesit* and her sister *Nub-nefert*; *Yb-Ymentet*; and *Yfert*] confirms the presence of a viable colony with Egyptian-type afterlife beliefs. Females would not have been chance members of a ship's crew.[69] The personages are generally identified by name and ancestry. Two are identified by trade - the scribe *Teta-ty* and the coppersmith *Ankef*. The importance given to these two individuals may reflect their status in the community, the latter arresting to the importance of a metallurgical technology.

No. 299: Round-topped limestone stele. Presented to the British Museum by J.B. Collings, 1836. Date, late XII dynasty.	At the top of the shen-sign between two sacred eyes. To left a male figure, seated, holding lotus; in front of him a woman standing and pouring a libation. Above the man is his name, *Thuy*: above the woman, *Yb-Ymentet*. Below are three horizontal lines of inscription:- 1. *May Osiris, this Ruler of eternity, give a royal offering. 2. May he give funeral offerings of bread and beer, oxen and birds (for) the ka of Thuy.* 3. (illegible)

---

[69] C. Testa, n.d.: op. cit.

No. 233: Round-topped limestone stele, now in the British Museum. Date, late XII dynasty (1991-1786 BCE).

Upper register: Vertical cartouche, "*The good god, Ne-maat-Re*". On the right, couchant jackal on perch holding ankl, three vertical lines of hieroglyphics. "*Beloved of Wep-wawet, lord of the necropolis*". On the left, standing figure of Osiris holding was-sceptre and ankh, two vertical lines of hieroglyphs, "*Beloved of Khenti-Amentiu, lord of Adbydos*". Ten horizontal lines of inscription:- 1. "*O ye who live upon earth, every wab-priest, every lector-priest, every scribe, every ka-servant. 2. who pass by this endowed stele forever: ye who love your life and your king, 3. ye who praise your city-gods, ye who transmit your offices to your children, 4. say ye, May Osiris, lord of Abdyos, give royal offering (may he give the funeral offering of bread and beer, oxen and birds, alabasters and linen, incense and perfume), 5. All things good and pure, which heaven gives, which the earth produces, which the Nile brings, and on which the god lives, 6. (a) For the ka of the coppersmith Ankef, born of Kenyuyt, (b) for the ka of Yfart, born of Ameny, 7. (a) for the ka of Yupy, born of Yfert, (b) for the ka of Meres-Tekh, born of Yf(ert), 8. (a) for the ka of Atet, born of Yfert, (b) for the ka of N..... 9. (a) for the ka of Senenu, born of ..... 10 (a) for the ka of R......*

91

No. 218: Round-topped stele, lower part broken away. Date XII dynasty.	At the top, shen-sign between two sacred eyes. To the left a woman kneeling on a low chair and holding a lotus; above is her name *Harem-hesit*. In front of her is a table of offerings. Facing her is a standing woman, over who is the inscription: "*by her sister who causes her name to live, Nub-nefert.*" Below one horizontal line of inscription remains: "*May Osiris, Ruler of eternity, give royal offering. May he give the funeral offerings of bread and beer, oxen and birds, and all things....*"
No. 287: Broken limestone stele. Presented to the British Museum by J.B. Collings, 1836. Date, early XVIII dynasty (1567-1320 BCE).	Figure of enthroned Osiris, below whom is a table of offerings and kneeling worshipper. Below are three horizontal lines of inscription: 1. *May Osiris Khenti-Amentiu (give a royal offering), may he give the sweet breezes to the north*, 2. *cool water, wine, milk, alabasters, linen..... all things good and pure*, 3. *for the ka of the scribe Teta-ty, justified, lord of worth.*"

An earlier controversial Egyptian-style find was a statue allegedly discovered accidentally in a solitary spot at Gozo in 1713. The statue was noted by Public Library curator in 1872 to have been found "*buried under rubbish which from time immemorial had accumulated there*".[70] The statue, or a similar one, was earlier mentioned by Charles S. Sonnini in 1791 who described it as "*An*

---

[70] C. Vassallo: A Guide to the Museum or the Ancient Monuments of Malta preserved in the Museum of the Public Library. Government Printing Office, Malta, 1872, p.13-14

antique statue in the hands of an Italian monk of the congregation of the Propaganda, who made a present of it to M. Tott. This statue, which is rather more than a foot in height is of white calcareous stone and was found at Thebies". He also included a diagrammatic picture of the statue.[71] The find was next mentioned by William Tallack in 1861 who commented that it was made of Maltese stone.[72] [22]. Cesare Vassallo in 1872 described it as "*an Egyptian triad borne by a Talamifera ……… carved in Malta stone, one foot two inches high, on a stand measuring six and a half inches on each side, and five and a half inches high. Osiris sits on a chair: he has human limbs with the head of an Ibis, and has the mysterious Tau on his shoulder. In the head of the Ibis is a small cavity in which the Mitre might have been placed with security. Isis, in female form, sits on the left, with the head-dress, the falls of which cover the breast on each side. She is enveloped in a close-fitting dress which descends to the heels, and the small cavity in the head indicates that at one time the usual embellishment of the lotus flower was not wanting. Orus is in the middle with a large disc on his falcon head. The Talamifera, which holds the chair, stands upright on her feet, covered from the waist downwards with a light skirt, and has the hair curled, not unlike that of the Egyptian female in Montfaucon's plate 140, number*

---

[71] C.S. Sonnini: Voyage dans la Haute et Basse Égypte, fait par ordre de l'ancien gouvernement et contenant des observations de tous genres. Avec une Collection de 40 Planches, gravées en taille-douce par J. P. P. Tardieu, contenant des Portraits, Vues, Plans, Carte Géographiques, Antiquités, Plantes, Animaux, etc. dessinnés sur les lieux, sous les yeux de l'Auteur. Buisson, Paris, cf plate XVIII.

[72] W. Tallack: Malta under the Phenicians, Knights and English. A.W. Bennett, London, 1861, p.135. Refers to the statue as one of the Egyptian remains found on the Islands, describing it as "a group of three figures (including Isis and Osiris), found in the island of Gozo, and bearing hieroglyphics on its surface. It is a point of peculiar interest that it is formed of Maltese stone." He also makes mention of several other statuettes decorated with hieroglyphics similar to those found with Egyptian mummies, and also records a 1694 find of some golden plates covered in Egyptian hieroglyphics that were presented to the Archbishop of Naples.

9. The sides of the pedestal and the square support immediately under the chair, as well as the stand, are enriched with hieroglyphics, as is likewise a band, in the shape of a ribbon, which, falling from the nape of the Talamifera, is lost in the stand." Dr. Lepsius studied the statue in 1842 with a view of deciphering the hieroglyphics.[73] A similar description was given by A.A. Caruana in 1882; while William K. Bedford published its first photographic depiction in 1894.[74] Temi Zammit in 1919 also described the statue as being "*of the type called Pastophori, or Talamophori, and represents a priest standing, with the figures of Horus, and Maet the Goddess of truth, with the moon disc between the two deities. The figures of Horus and Maet are also engraved on the shoulders of the priest. The inscription cut on the group is a prayer to Amen-Ra-Seker and Maet the great Goddess of Thebes, invoking the spirit of Neferinpet the priest, and a prayer to Ra-Harmachis and Maet, the lady of the skies*". He assigned the group to the 19th to 20th dynasties or about 1200 BCE.[75] Seker in Egyptian myth was a mummified hawk-headed god of the underworld who was eventually identified with Osiris. Harmakhis [or Hor-m-akhet] was the name given to the falcon-headed solar god Horus on the horizon. Maat was the lady of the heaven, queen of the earth and mistress of the underworld who symbolised justice. The depicted deities have been identified as the same ones mentioned in the hieroglyphics. This statue is presently housed in the Museum of Archaeology in Malta. It has been

---

[73] C. Vassallo, 1872: op. cit., p.13-14
[74] A.A. Caruana: Report of the Phoenician and Roman Antiquities of the Maltese Islands. Government Press, Malta, 1882; W.K. Bedford, 1894: op. cit., p.11-12, plate on pg.13
[75] T. Zammit, 1919: op. cit., p.43-44

proposed that this statue originated from Thebes in Egypt and was eventually deposited in the Maltese archaeological collection.[76]

Sepulchral statute
[providence: Gozo]
After: Bedford, 1894

Sepulchral statute
[providence: Thebes]
After: Sonnini, 1791

The above artefacts have been dated by common consensus to the second millennium BCE. These remains have unfortunately no definite archaeological context to assist dating. While the early local documentation suggests a Maltese provenance, this cannot be absolutely confirmed and the finds could easily be modern

---

[76] I. Vella Gregory: Neferaabet at the National Museum of Archaeology. The Sunday Times [Malta], 2nd November 2003, p.50-51

importations. However, the possibility of importation in antiquity cannot be absolutely ruled out.

Of more definite providence is the golden plate covered in Egyptian hieroglyphics which was excavated from a tomb in Gozo in 1694. This was eventually presented to the Archbishop of Naples. The item has been diagrammatically depicted in G.F. Abela and G. Ciantar in the work *Malta Illustrata* dated 1772.[77][27]. Attempts to trace this artefact have as yet been unsuccessful.

Gold plate with Egyptian hieroglyphics [providence: Gozo]
After: Abela and Ciantar, 1772

The evidence needs to be re-examined but it appears unlikely that an intrusive community with an Egyptian culture cohabited the islands with the Tarxien Cemetery Phase community. In the spirit of repatriation of cultural heritage to countries of origin, it may be opportune for the Maltese authorities to ask the British authorities to return the Bighi stele together with other important archaeological artefacts.

---

[77] G.F. Abela, G. Ciantar: *Malta Illustrata*. Malta, 1772

Classical sources on Mummification

Rhind Bilingual Papyrus

The First Part of the Papyrus

[Pl. I. lines 1-10] The year 13, the 28th of the month Athyr, of the reign of the monarch Ptolemaius the father-loving (Philopator III), was born a good son in the place of his father, the Ehem Sebau, so named. His father was the archon of the city of Southern Anna (Hermonthis), priest of Mentu, lord of Southern Annu (Hermonthis), Menkara by name for he was greatly beloved and much esteemed in the hearts of his brethren; what emanated from him was beloved, whatever he did is excellent to speak of. He left a son and daughter after him to offer. He passed 59 years, and entered upon the 60th year by 10 months and 14 days. Seated with millions there was made to him a good [Pl. II. lines 1-10] place of the scents of Pant (Phoenicia) constantly. There was not found evil in his heart in the festivals of each god when before him on the first day. The close of his life came, he was turned back, and strode into the Place of new Birth. He came out, and went into the Kar neter as if on earth. He went to the Place of Enwrapping in the 21st year of Caesar. The funeral was made from the 10th to the 15th Epiphi, clothed, prepared, and done in the region of Akar, by the scribes, servants of Ra was received by those in the Empyreal Gate, the gods of the land of He was washed, brother of the maha (cousin) of the king, the Ehem Sebau, the son of the divine builder, the priest of Mentu, lord of Southern Annu (Hermonthis), Menkara, born of Tapamentu.

[Pl. III. lines 1-10] The 10th Epiphi was the Purification on the whole earth. His form wished to proceed to the heaven directly .... It was not sent to the Place of new Birth daily, it was purified, it did not pass the Pool .... the funeral in ail places at their time. It was at *rest in the Plants (?) of the good Fields; it made its transformations, it had the place in a moment, victorious against the enemies of the Eyes on the first day. He is not seen by Osiris humiliating the limbs emanating from him, prepared through the words passed by Anubis, going as those never at rest to [Bu] Sta. His heart follows all other things. Thou comest with the concealed ones at the close of millions. Thy soul comes forth as a phoenix, thy heart appears as a hawk, an ibis is in thy body, as a kite and as a vulture, flying like the [Pl. IV. lines 1-8] soul of the great Bull. Oh! the good one who has gone to repose; oh! the good one who goes round the pylons of the horizon. I place thy arms on thy belly, as was done to father Osiris. Thy arms (or limbs) are prepared by him who is on the Hill, under the form of the chief of the funeral. A road for thy impurity is made in the ocean, for thy impurity is given to the winds, Amset rejoices to embalm him. Hapi delights to obliterate his faults. Tuautmutf delights at the healing of his faults. Kabhsnuf rejoices that he has passed from the Place of Preparation. Thy arms are laid out, made in the shape of the arms of the Osiris, brother of the maha (cousin) of the king, [the Khem Sebau,] son of the priest of Mentu, lord of Southern Annu (Hermonthis), Menkara, born of the lady of the house Tapamentu!*

[Pl. V. lines 1-10] Thou comest forth rejoicing from the Place of Punishment, for thou hast thrown open the Annu, for after the 36 days thou camest forth. I steeped thee in the great Pool of Chonsu, in peace behind the Rusta in the region of the West, opening Annu at the 30th (?) day. Passing their arms to the god, the four born of Horus placed their hands (?) on his head. The legs, the two arms, the waist, the back were at rest for 30 days in the Place of Washing of Isis the great mother. She took care to make the good funeral of the brother of the house, Khem [usher] Sebau, son of the priest of Monta Ra, lord of Southern Annu (Hermonthis), Menkara, born of Tapamentu, who was boiled in 200 jars of salt, also in frankincense, anointed with oil by Horus, lord of the Tomb ... [Pl. VI. lines 1-10] m has wrapped him in his divine linen. Thy (his) limbs are wrapped in the fabrics of the gods and goddesses. Annp prepares the

decoration of thy sarcophagus, and with the jars of menni which the gods produce in the East, and cedar oil ... steeped again in (?) delicious essence of noble balm, fragrance in ail thy limbs. Thy body is enclosed in the best fabrics, coming forth at first to see the youthful Sun when he lifts his beauties from the Pool on the 26th of Mesori. Thou hast been equipped with ail the decorations of the Osirian brother divine usher (?) Sebau, son of the governor of Southern Annu (Hermonthis), priest of Mentn, lord of Southern Annu (Hermonthis), Menkara, the name of whose mother is Tapamentu.

[Pl. VII. lines 1-10] I am the preparer of the road before ail coming to the Place of the poorly clad. I prepare the path for all who tread in the Hall of the two Truths. He is chief of the Place; son of the chief of the soldiers in Southern Annu (Hermonthis), priest of Mentu, lord of Southern Annu (Hermonthis), Menkara, the name of whose mother is Tapamentu. I pass thy words before the lord of the West; thou hast beheld the light, at the raising of his beauties. I declare thy virtues before his two sisters. I declare thy praise amongst the prepared spirits. I hail thy form in the Rusta, in the abode of Oa-mut. [Pl. VIII. lines 1-10] Thou hast been allowed to be fabricated in thy house daily. After thou art let to be prepared in thy city, thou art enshrouded in all beauty thou wishest, without diminution in thy time, not doing any evil in thy day. Thou hast ruled on earth; thy house was open, no evil was said in it daily. Thou hast ranged through the Hades for thy heart, seeking for it everywhere, thy limbs are weary through the work. Thou walkest in the Gateway of the Horizon while thou passest thy time; thou art clad as a person in white, for the good things thou hast done on earth; thou hast been given leisure (or a 'tomb') in Hades. Thou hast had a salted embalmment, and linen fabrics for thy limbs of the best linen. Anap has prepared thee in thy coffin, thy soul flourishes in thy body in thy house, thou livest again in thy sepulchre, thou goest and comest before the lord of Eternity.

[Pl. IX. lines 1-10] The great god opens his mouth, his words come in peace following him; his things remain daily. Thou passest thy time in it, thou hast gone after Astennu, thou followest to the Place of the Horizon, gleaming in gold, a great god, augmenting his form. The breath of living again comes, making thee behold peace for ever after. Thou hast passed thy years, thou hast closed thy time of a good life; thou treadest in the region of the breath of life, thou breathest in it and remainest in thy sepulture or thy apartment within thy house; thou art renewed as the gods dwelling there, thou hast opened the good Place of the close of Millions, thou hast the divine beat of Kar neter (Hades). Thou adorest the lord of Eternity with his sister Isis, kissing his face; thou prostratest thyself all round the place, [Pl. X. lines 1-10] giving glory where the lord of Eternity is. Thou turnest thy face to the region of the hidden ones in Kar neter (Hades); thou honourest the lord who watches millions of the Land of Life; thou makest adoration to his good face, adoring the excellent one at rest in his good place; he gives thy spirit its breath. Thou addressest thy prayers to the chief of the gods and men; he gives thy soul to pass into thy body, to speak as thou didst before, to dwell in all the places where the gods are. The gods of the Orbits adore thee, saying thou art the best of prepared spirits; they rejoice to see thy form, rising in its shapes, dressed in linen. Thy limbs are enwrapt by the work of Anal, salted by the arms of Am, passing the doors of the Hall of the two Truths; thy fore and hinder parts are mummied like the gods in their shapes. Oh! Osirian brother, Sebau, son of Menkara, priest of Mentu, born of Tapamentu.

[Pl. XI. lines 1-11] The chapter of the Purification made by Horus and Thoth. Horus says thou art purified at thy going in Hades or the gateway of the Ta-ser, to see that great god in Hades. There is not any evil in thee, Thoth hath dipped thee, thou art dressed in thy bandages, all thy limbs are salted. There is nothing revolting to a god in thee; there is no pollution in thy limbs. Thou hast been washed in the waters which emanate from Abu (Elephantine), with the things (?) of Horus which come from Nubu (Syene), with the milk

(?) of Kami. Thy soul lives like the lord of Grief, thy body like the soul above. Thy limbs are excellent like those of Unnefer, thy mummy is set up like Samaut. Thou hast been received in the Hall of the two Truths. Thy soul comes out to the heaven with Orion, and the stars in the train of the Dog-star; they let thee breathe the air within thy envelope, thy lungs breathe the breath of life; they let thy teeth chatter in thy chest like the fly coming from the end of the nostril of life, giving thee thy place (or throne) like the secret fire under the flame, living again at the nostril of the Cycle. Thou goest and comest before the meek-hearted; thou receivest libations at the hands of Isis and Nephthys. Thou art placed on thy tomb in front of . . . as. The heaven under the form of Athor, regent of the West, gives her arms to receive thee. [Pl. XII. lines 1-10] Thou goest backwards every ten days. Thy soul lives of the flux which emanates from Osiris to the arms of Amenapt. Thou passest into the Hades daily to receive the cakes in the hands, coming forth peaceably from Gammut by the aid of Chonsu, in Gam Neferhept, saying thou hast glorified thy father and mother, thou hast glorified thy brethren, thy heart is washed, thy limbs are washed. The Osirian brother, divine Sebau, son of the governor of Southern Annu (Hermonthis), priest of Mentu, lord of Southern Annu, Menkara, son of Tapamentu.

[Pl. XIII. lines 1-10] Hail the one placed upon earth, going to the end of time, a long time on earth with a good life, not giving evil transmigrations of life in thy heart. The little babe ... when it went to Hades. Thy shape is thy power on earth, thon obtainest thy victories by it. Thou doest ail things thy heart wishes. All beings are prostrate before thee; no falsehood is said before thee daily, because the head of the earth thou hast trod in it; the great child who guards the ...., the chief of gods and men, the greatest of the gods of the Empyreal Gate, the divine Creator of the gods, their chief, ordering the navigation, leading along the gods. Mayst thou rejoice with the wise spirits! Thou art with the servants of Osiris, they adore (?) thy body seeing thy beauty; thou art enrolled among the ministers of Osiris. Thou criest with a loud voice: [Pl. XIV. lines 1-10] "Hail, my father,

Osiris! I am one making his heart, I did no wicked crime, there is no fault in me, hating thy form in my time. Truth was diffused through my heart, I gave bread to him who was destitute, I eating the food before me. I stand before Astennu, I have bent down in the Land of the lord of the Weight and guardian of the Balance, I stand before the two Truths as one very excellent before them. My form returns to serve, my form is as the great blessed of the Gate of the Ta-ser. Thou beholdest thy father Sochsris-Osiris on the morning of the festival of Socharis in the Gate; at thy glorifications he has received thee with delight, the Osiris brother of the Khem Sebauf, son of the governor of Southern Annu (Hermonthis), priest of Mentu Ra, lord of Southern Annu (Hermonthis), Menkara, son of Tapamentu.

[Pl. XV. lines 1-10] The Book of the Transmigrations of Thoth to protect thee. Thou art not turned back from the Hall of Osiris. Thou risest at morning from the cabin, in the faces of all men come to see thee; thou sittest in the hind cabin at evening, all men and women adore thee. Thou hast tied the pendant with all precious stones, silver and gold innumerable. Thy soul comes forth from heaven, it adores the Sun when he rises. Thou receivest this writing made by Astennu, when he went from the Gate of the Empyreal region. Thou livest for ever; thou reachest the first Hall of the West, led by the gods giving thee a road. Horus and A (Thoth) purify thee going in peace; for the principal gods of the Empyreal region adore thy approach to the house of him who dwells in the West, magnifying thy preparation before all men. The four children of Horus [Pl. XVI. lines 1-10] are before thee adoring the lord of Eternity; their arms turn back to his face. Amset, Hapy Tuaatmutf, Kabhsennf, say: we come to our father when he approaches the Kar neter, or Hades; he did no evil in his day. We drink of the waters daily, we eat its fowl and its fish as our hearts wish. We feed off the best and repose on the best. We make the place of those who are before us. We grow old on earth, we tread the Hades, we declare his goodness before the lord of the Empyreal region. He listens to our words, the lord of the West. Thou art praised for ever, thou art made for ever, he lets thee *flourish in thy closed house. The Osiris brother, loyal watcher of the stud, the Khem Sebauf, son of the governor of Southern Annu, priest of Mentu, Menkara, son of Tapamentu.*

[Pl. XVII. lines 1-10] That great god opens his mouth to the words of the gods, at peace through them his heart is correct. May he follow orders! May his soul go forth to heaven with the other souls! May his body remain in the Empyreal Gate! He has had given to him food off the table daily. Isis turns and says to Nephthys, rejoicing her face. The gods of the Gateway also give divine offerings to the Osirian divine brother, Khem Sebauf, son of the chief of the soldiers in Southern Annu (Hermonthis), priest of Mentu, lord of Southern Annu (Hermonthis), Menkara, born of Tapamentu. Osiris who dwells in the West, great god, lord of Abydos; Socharis-Osiris who dwells in the void; Isis the great mother-goddess and Nephthys the sister-goddess; Annp who dwells in the divine hall and is attached to the embalmment, lord of Ta-ser.

[Pl. XVIII. lines 1-10] The gods of the two Truths in the great hall, the gods of the orbit who traverse the Empyreal region, the great wise spirits of the Hades, the gods and goddesses give meals of food and drink, oxen and geese, wine and milk, incense and salt, bread, grain, corn, and food, all good things off which a god lives, for the Osirian divine brother, standard-bearer Sebauf, son of the lord, the chief commander of troops in Southern Annu (Hermonthis), priest of Menkara, lord of Southern Annu (Hermonthis), Menkara, born of Tapamentu. The light of the Sun shines upon his body, its rays follow his divine limbs, his soul goes to the heaven and follows the disk, he is united with the followers of Osiris, he is ... in his service. He left a son and a daughter to offer after him, he does not fail on earth for ever.

[Pl. XIX. lines 1-10] Oh, gods and goddesses unmentionable! ascribe ye the truth, obliterate ye the faults of the Osirian divine brother, Khem Sebauf, son of the governor of the city, prophet of

Southern Annu (Hermonthis), Menkara, the name of whose mother was Tapamenta, justified. Place ye the heart in his chest, open ye his eyes, and close his mouth, give passage to his nostrils, make his arms as strong as those of Unnefer, let his soul go forth to heaven where it wishes to be, let him not be turned away from any region in which he wishes to be. May his body be daily as the universal lord! His heart is in all places in which his existence wishes to be. Oh, Son! oh, Atum! oh, Shu! oh, Tefnu! oh, Seb! oh, Nu! oh, Osiris! oh, Isis! oh, Nephthys! oh, Horus! oh, Athor! oh, greater gods! Oh, lesser gods! oh, Never at rest! Oh, Incorruptible! oh, Constellation of the Southern heaven! [Pl. XX. lines 1-11] oh, Birthplace star of the northern heaven! oh, Dog-star, ruler of stars! Bast, great lady of (Bu) Bastis! great Tat! great Boat! Athor, regent of the West! Seb, lord of the gods! Thoth, lord of Truth, Bull in the West! guard ye the Osiris divine brother, the Khem Sebauf, son of the chief of the city, priest of Mentu, lord of Southern Annu, Menkara, born of Tapamenta; tie your charms on him, let him come forth justified, give delicious breath to his nostril daily, that he may do what he wishes wherever he goes. By the words of Ra the great god in his disk, or the words of Isis the great mother-goddess, the god of the Sun in his own name, ordered is what he bas said, all that proceeds out of his mouth is done forthwith.

[Pl. XXI. lines 1-10] The Osirian divine brother, Khem Sebauf, son of the divine workman of Southern Annu (Hermonthis), Mentu, priest of Mentu Ra, lord of Southern Annu (Hermonthis), Menkara, born of Tapamentu, living for ever. His soul flourishes at the rising and setting, like the subjects of the gods in their time who have a place in the abode of the lord of the gods daily; his name is heard of in the Place of the gods, who give breath to his person daily. The paintings of thy mother Nupe are within the abode, having come in peace to dwell in thy chest. The abode of thy heart is eternal. My arms enfold to embrace thy limbs, protecting thy body, taking care of thy great mummy, giving life to thy soul for ever.

[Pl. XXII. lines 1-10] The Osirian divine brother, Khem Sebauf, son of the divine builder of Annu, Mentu, prophet of Mentu Ra, lord of Southern Annu (Hermonthis), Menkara, son of Tapamentu. The greater and lesser gods come to thee, to be thy protection, to watch over thy height and length, and to lead thee in thy sepulchre in Gammut. The children of Horus keep watch over thee by night and day continually. Thou art made young in thy length and bread by making to thee living charms as do those to him who dwells in the West, the great god, lord of the East, in the festivals of Socharis. The gods and spirits who pass the Gate have come to thee. Thou hast taken the good way to the West. *[Pl. XXIII. lines 1-9]* They open to thee the gates of the Empyreal region in the Western Horizon. Thou comest and goest out of it. They give thee drink and food off the altars of Osiris daily, they have, opened to thee the heaven rejoicing, Anap in the recesses of the Hall embalming thee. Thou goest with thy legs in the footwalks of Hades, as if thy wast upon earth, smiting the heads of thy enemies, justified before Osiris.

The Second Part of the Papyrus (Demotic)

[Pl. XXIV. lines 1-10] In the 19th year, the 26th of Pashons, of the ruler Ptolemy the living, a good day, was born in the house of her father and her mother a good person who was called Taani, daughter of the lord chief prophet of Mentu, lord of Southern Annu (Hermonthis), a great chief before men, Kalasher, born of the Athorian Aiut, they were her father and mother. She was the lady of the house of the brother of the mahau of the ruler, Mentu-Sebauf, son of Menkara. She was the good nurse of her son in his house, and reverenced for what she did (?). She made her existence in life still she completed her age of 54 years, was ....

[Pl. XXV. lines 1-13] On the 21st year the 28th Mesori, the day of the reign of Caesar was complete ... was the evil day of the being on earth of the daughter of the archon in Southern Annu

(Hermonthis), Taani the wife of the divine architect [?] of Annu and Mentu (Hermonthis), the priest of Mentu, lord of Southern Annu (Hermonthis), brother of the king's mahau, Kalasher, son of Menkara, child of the Athorian lady Aiut. A place in the region of Akar was ordered to be made for her; she was enrolled in the Empyreal regions by the title which is in heaven and on earth, having her age amongst gods and men, under her true title of reverencing what was ordered of the gods, hating iniquity, honouring what was commanded a true being. The embalmment of the wife of the royal officer of Southern Annu (Hermonthis), the brother of the guardian of the king, Taani, daughter of Kalasher, born of the Athorian Aiut, was made.

[Pl. XXVI. lines 1-12] Approaching the Akar, was survivor of her husband for 48 days, going the Washing-place at the end of the time. The inscription was engraved on the coffin of the deceased. All the forms were done for bearing her in the Place of Truth, all in the .... opened at their time. I come forth rejoicing as the day, rowed by ... of the great Pool of Chonsu, all my limbs steeped in the Washing-place by the work of Anup who belongs to the embalmment and its lord of the Chief of Ta-ser, who adorned my muscles, who made my skin united, who fashioned my bones, who made my arms youthful in the Gate of the Horizon. The good lady Taani, wife of Kalasher, born of the Athorian Aiut, mistress of the house of the brother of the royal mahau Mentu-Sebauf.

[Pl. XXVII. lines 1-6] She turns back to Isis. She was buried as or by the daughter of her father. The lady Taani, the daughter of the brother of the mahau of the great house (king) Kalashbi, born of the Athorian Aiut, lady of the house (wife) of the brother of the mahau of the great house Mentu-Sebauf. She was prepared in salt at Mut; she was prepared in bitumen, frankincense, and in the Hall of the West, by Horus lord of the sepulchral chamber; Sahem tied her with his divine fingers. Thy limbs were wrapped in the fabric of the gods and goddesses, Anup prepared thee by steeping thy limbs in salt and

linen. I come forth, my body is adorned with the ornaments and in the type of the goddess Athor, the ruler of the West. I see the young Sun raising his beauties, lost in his waters on the 26th of the month Choiak; he orders me, receives me a prepared [spirit].

[Pl. XXVIII. lines 1-10] Anup attached to the embalmment, lord of Ta-ser, arranges the path before me to the Halls of the clothing the Naked [?], he arranges for me a good path to the Hall of the two Truths, he makes me flourish in all places for ever he makes me one of the followers of the mistress of the West, to go transported into the Ra, and remain for ever placed in Rusta in the abode of Gammat, prepared in Abat daily. The Athorian .... Hannunefer, daughter of the lady Taani, daughter of the guardian of the body-guard mahau of the king Kalusharan, son of the lord the chief, the prophet of Mentu, lord of Southern Annu (Hermonthis), Menkara, and born of the Athorian Aiut, daughter of the lady of the house of the guardian of the mahau of the king Mentu-Sebauf, in peace, breathing, and living again in the tomb daily.

[Pl. XXIX. lines 1-12] She comes in peace, one of the hailed, in the Land of Life, after the termination of her time of good life in the given only a son and daughter to offer after her. We are watching the coming into her of the breath of life in the Land of Life, united with the female followers of Athor, regent of the West, opening the good house of the close of millions. My forepart meets the coming of the lord of the West. His two sisters are with him; Anubis adoring his face, honouring his .... for ever and ever. He has renewed me, and says he gives my soul, by the breath or transmigrations, in my body; he gives breath in all my limbs, as if I had the breath of life. Taani, daughter of the brother of the mahau of the lady, Kalasher, child of the Athorian Aiut, lady of the house of the brother of the mahau of the king Mentu-Sebauf.

[Pl. XXX. lines 1-10] The Athorian daughter, lady Taani, daughter of the brother of the mahau of the king Kalasheran, son of the Athorian Aiut, lady of the house of the brother of the mahau of the king Mentu-Sebauf. The goddess Nu gives her arms to take thee in her shape of Athor, the regent of the West; she lets thee see Socharis-Osiris on the morning of the festival of Socharis. Isis the great mother, Nephthys the sister-goddess, Anupa who dwells in the divine Gateway, Anupu who is attached to the embalmment over the region of Ta-ser, the gods and goddesses who are in Gammut, the prepared spirits who are in Rusta in face of the lord of Asti, ail the gods say to thee adoring, we grant thee to go in and go out of the Hall of Truth; thy soul to live with the souls in heaven, thy body to remain in Abat daily.

[Pl. XXXI. lines 1-10] The Book of the Lamentations made by Astennu, in order not to be turned back from the Hall of Osiris. I rise at morning in the cabin to all men; I come and am seen; I set in the cabin at evening, male and female make adoration. I have transported safe in the great house, their silver, gold, and numerous clothes. My soul comes forth to heaven, to see the son when he shines ... This inscription which Astennu made for me to go in the door of the Gateway, led by the guides of the roads. Horus and Thoth purify thee, going in peace like the great gods who are in the Gateway, adoring thee .... approaching the gate of the West, to the great fabricator of men, declared happy before the lord of the West. I am praised for ever, made for ever. He lets my body remain in the tomb daily. [Pl. XXXII. lines 1-5] The Athorian lady, Taani, daughter of the brother of the .... of the king Kalasherau, born of the Athorian Aiut.

The great god he opens his mouth to speak to the other gods, at peace is his own face; he orders Hannunefer, her heart is ready. May she be placed as the chief of the servants of the lord of Eternity! May her soul come forth with the souls, her body remains in the Gateway of the heaven!

[Pl. XXXIII. lines 1-10] His sister Isis says to Nephthys, Rejoice over her, oh gods of the Gateway! as over the prepared dead who are in Gammut. The Athorian has the breath of life, may she be with you in Rusta in Gammut! May she be united with the servants of the two sisters, [and have] meals of food and drink, wine, milk, wax, supplies of food, and all things good and pure off which a god lives! To the Athorian Taani, daughter of the brother of the mahau of the king, Kalasherau, son of Menkara, born of the Athorian Aiut.

Anubis, God of Embalming and Guide and Friend of the Dead

Herodotus

The mode of embalming, according to the most perfect process, is the following:- They take first a crooked piece of iron, and with it draw out the brain through the nostrils, thus getting rid of a portion, while the skull is cleared of the rest by rinsing with drugs; next they make a cut along the flank with a sharp Ethiopian stone, and take out the whole contents of the abdomen, which they then cleanse, washing it thoroughly with palm wine, and again frequently with an infusion of pounded aromatics. After this they fill the cavity with the purest bruised myrrh, with cassia, and every other sort of spicery except frankincense, and sew up the opening. Then the body is placed in natrum for seventy days, and covered entirely over. After the expiration of that space of time, which must not be exceeded, the body is washed, and wrapped round, from head to foot, with bandages of fine linen cloth, smeared over with gum, which is used generally by the Egyptians in the place of glue, and in this state it is given back to the relations, who enclose it in a wooden case which they have had made for the purpose, shaped into the figure of a man. Then fastening the case, they place it in a sepulchral chamber, upright against the wall. Such is the most costly way of embalming the dead.

If persons wish to avoid expense, and choose the second process, the following is the method pursued:- Syringes are filled with oil made from the cedar-tree, which is then, without any incision or disembowelling, injected into the abdomen. The passage by which it might be likely to return is stopped, and the body laid in natrum the prescribed number of days. At the end of the time the cedar-oil is allowed to make its escape; and such is its power that it brings with it the whole stomach and intestines in a liquid state. The natrum meanwhile has dissolved the flesh, and so nothing is left of the dead body but the skin and the bones. It is returned in this condition to the relatives, without any further trouble being bestowed upon it.

The third method of embalming, which is practised in the case of the poorer classes, is to clear out the intestines with a clyster, and let the body lie in natrum the seventy days, after which it is at once given to those who come to fetch it away.

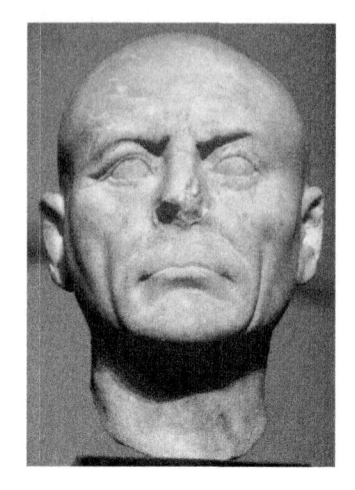

Diodorus Siculus

91 1 But not least will a man marvel at the peculiarity of the customs of the Egyptians when he learns of their usages with respect to the dead. For whenever anyone dies among them, all his relatives and friends, plastering their heads with mud, roam about the city lamenting, until the body receives burial. Nay more, during that time they indulge in neither baths, nor wine, nor in any other food worth mentioning, nor do they put on bright clothing. 2 There are three classes of burial, the most expensive, the medium, and the most humble. And if the first is used the cost, they say, is a talent of silver, if the second, twenty minae, and if the last, the expense is, they say, very little indeed. 3 Now the men who treat the bodies are skilled artisans who have received this professional knowledge as a family tradition; and these lay before the relatives of the deceased a price-list of every item connected with the burial, and ask them in what manner they wish the body to be treated. 4 When an agreement has been reached on every detail and they have taken the body, they turn it over to men who have been assigned to the service and have become inured to it. The first is the scribe, as he is called, who, when the body has been laid on the ground, circumscribes on the left flank the extent of the incision; then the one called the slitter37 cuts the flesh, as the law commands, with an Ethiopian stone38 and at once takes to flight on the run, while those present set out after him, pelting him with stones, heaping curses on him, and trying, as it were, to turn the profanation on his head; for in their eyes everyone is an object of general hatred who applies violence to the body of a man of the same tribe or wounds him or, in general, does him any harm.

5 The men called embalmers, however, are considered worthy of every honour and consideration, associating with the priests and even coming and going in the temples without hindrance, as being undefiled. When they have gathered to treat the body after it has been slit open, one of them thrusts his hand through the opening in the corpse into the trunk and extracts everything but the kidneys and heart, and another one cleanses each of the viscera, washing them in palm wine and spices. 6 And in general, they carefully dress the whole body for over thirty days, first with cedar oil and certain other preparations, and then with myrrh, cinnamon, and such spices as have the faculty not only of preserving it for a long time but also of giving it a fragrant odour. And after treating the body they return it to the relatives of the deceased, every member of it having been so preserved intact that even the hair on the eyelids and brows remains, the entire appearance of the body is unchanged, and the cast of its shape is recognizable. 7 This explains why many Egyptians keep the bodies of their ancestors in costly chambers and gaze face to face upon those who died many generations before their own birth, so that, as they look upon the stature and proportions and the features of the countenance of each, they experience a strange enjoyment, as though they had lived with those on whom they gaze.

92 When the body is ready to be buried the family announces the day of interment to the judges and to the relatives and friends of the deceased, and solemnly affirms that he who has just passed away — giving his name — "is about to cross the lake." 2 Then, when the judges, forty-two in number, 39 have assembled and have taken seats

113

in a hemicycle which has been built across the lake, the baris40 is launched, which has been prepared in advance by men especially engaged in that service, and which is in the charge of the boatman whom the Egyptians in their language charon.41 3 For this reason they insist that Orpheus, having visited Egypt in ancient times and witnessed this custom, merely invented his account of Hades, in part reproducing this practice and in part inventing on his own account; but this point we shall discuss more fully a little later.42 4 At any rate, after the baris has been launched into the lake but before the coffin containing the body is set in it, the law gives permission to anyone who wishes to arraign the dead person. Now if anyone presents himself and makes a charge, and shows that the dead man had led an evil life, the judges announce the decision to all and the body is denied the customary burial; but if it shall appear that the accuser has made an unjust charge he is severely punished. 5 When no accuser appears or the one who presents himself is discovered to be a slanderer, the relatives put their mourning aside and laud the deceased. And of his ancestry, indeed, they say nothing, as the Greeks do, since they hold that all Egyptians are equally well born, but after recounting his training and education from childhood, they describe his righteousness and justice after he attained to manhood, also his self-control and his other virtues, and call upon the gods of the lower world to receive him into the company of the righteous; and the multitude shouts its assent and extorts the glory of the deceased, as of one who is about to spend eternity in Hades among the righteous. 6 Those who have private sepulchers lay the body in a vault reserved for it, but those who possess none construct a new chamber in their own home, and stand the coffin upright against the firmest wall. Any also who are forbidden burial because of the accusations brought against them or because their bodies have been made security for a loan they lay away in their own homes; and it sometimes happens that their sons' sons, when they have become prosperous and paid off the debt or cleared them of the charges, give them later a magnificent funeral.

93 1 It is a most sacred duty, in the eyes of the Egyptians, that they should be seen to honour their parents or ancestors all the more after they have passed to their eternal home. Another custom of theirs is to put up the bodies of their deceased parents as security for a loan; and failure to repay such debts is attended with the deepest disgrace as well as with deprivation of burial at death. 2 And a person may well admire the men who established these customs, because they strove to inculcate in the inhabitants, as far as was possible, virtuousness and excellence of character, by means not only of their converse with the living but also of their burial and affectionate care of the dead. 3 For the Greeks have handed down their beliefs in such matters — in the honour paid to the righteous and the punishment of the wicked — by means of fanciful tales and discredited legends; consequently, these accounts not only cannot avail to spur their people on to the life, but, on the contrary, being scoffed at by worthless men, are received with contempt. 4 But among the Egyptians, since these matters do not belong to the realm of myth but men see with their own eyes that punishment is meted out to the wicked and honour to the good, every day of their lives both the wicked and the good are reminded of their obligations and in this way the greatest and most profitable amendment of men's characters is affected. And the best laws, in my opinion, must be held to be, not those by which men become most prosperous, but those by which they become most virtuous in character and best fitted for citizenship.

Porphyry

10. This also, no less than the above-mentioned particulars, induced them to believe, that animals should be reverenced [as images of the Gods], viz. that the soul of every animal, when liberated from the body, was discovered by them to be rational, to be prescient of futurity, to possess an oracular power, and to be effective of everything which man is capable of accomplishing when separated from the body. Hence, they very properly honoured them, and abstained from them as much as possible. Since, however, the cause through which the Egyptians venerated the Gods through animals requires a copious discussion, and which would exceed the limits of the present treatise, what has been unfolded respecting this particular is sufficient for our purpose. Nevertheless, this is not to be omitted, that the Egyptians, when they buried those that were of noble birth, privately took away the belly and placed it in a chest, and together with other things which they performed for the sake of the dead body, they elevated the chest towards the sun, whom they invoked as a witness; an oration for the deceased being at the same time made by one of those to whose care the funeral was committed. But the oration which Euphantus has interpreted from the Egyptian tongue was as follows: "O Sovereign Sun, and all ye Gods who impart life

to men, receive me, and deliver me to the eternal Gods as a cohabitant. For I have always piously worshipped those divinities which were pointed out to me by my parents as long as I lived in this age, and have likewise always honoured those who procreated my body. And, with respect to other men, I have never slain any one, nor defrauded any one of what he deposited with me, nor have I committed any other atrocious deed. If, therefore, during my life I have acted erroneously, by eating or drinking things which it is unlawful to eat or drink, I have not erred through myself, but through these," pointing to the chest in which the belly was contained. And having thus spoken, he threw the chest into the river [Nile]; but buried the rest of the body as being pure. After this manner, they thought an apology ought to be made to divinity for what they had eaten and drank, and for the insolent conduct which they had been led to through the belly.

Printed in Great Britain
by Amazon